Marketing Power for Financial Advisors

How to Attract a Predictable Flow of Your
Ideal Clients for a More Rewarding Practice

Bob Hanson and Shirley Hanson

authorHOUSE®

AuthorHouse™
1663 Liberty Drive
Bloomington, IN 47403
www.authorhouse.com
Phone: 1-800-839-8640

Published by AuthorHouse 09/30/2014

ISBN: 978-1-4969-3178-8 (sc)
ISBN: 978-1-4969-3177-1 (hc)
ISBN: 978-1-4969-3176-4 (e)

Library of Congress Control Number: 2014913884

For more marketing power from Bob Hanson
and Shirley Hanson, visit
MarketingPlanFinancialAdvisor.com

Contents

Chapter 1

This Could Be You

You may have said something like this: "The only thing I lack in my financial advisory practice is marketing to develop a prospect flow; then I could double my practice easily." Or, perhaps, you said, "I know I need to specialize, but I am not sure where to start." You see yourself as just another look-alike advisor, with an all-things-to-all-people approach.

Or you may fall into the category of many advisors who try to select marketing programs or tactics *before* they understand their market or grasp the message that will resonate with their audience. As a result, you are stuck with a hit-or-miss marketing program that wastes your resources.

Or, possibly, you count on only one way of reaching your market, which can derail your chance of achieving your goals.

Or you may expect branding—your logo, company name, and a slogan—to kindle your marketing momentum.

You may have spent years or even decades building your practice up to this point, and you are looking for a smart road map to double assets under management. You may feel that you are throwing money heedlessly at marketing, and you don't want to squander your resources on trial and error.

We Wrote This Book for You

We unleash our experience over our combined 46 years in marketing to give you a *streamlined system* that propels you to your desired results. The cost-effective strategies and time-tested tactics you discover here will eliminate the frustrations of random, unpredictable marketing. They prevent time-wasting dead ends and detours.

To help you to get off to a fast start we organized the book around the 3 P's of *Planning* (and its seven steps), *Packaging* (your core communications that tell your story), and *Promoting* (high-gain marketing tools). The chapters on "Getting Into Your Growth Groove" enable you to build a sound foundation for the growth you are looking for.

Our goal is to unlock the power of marketing leverage through a clear-cut system you can call on again and again. This system takes you directly to the strategies and tools that will make the most difference in your practice. You receive exactly what you need when you need it to boost your flow of new prospects and "A" clients. Above all, we want to inspire you as you go along your personal path to a more rewarding and fulfilling practice.

What's Behind the System?

Over the years, some individuals have brought particular expertise in marketing to the advisor growth challenge and the problem of attracting a stream of ideal prospects. They may have carried out primary research through numerous interviews on what is working for high-growth advisory practices.

Others have sought solutions from other industries and introduced those to financial advisors. And others have followed in detail what worked for a single practice over many market cycles, created a playbook, and shared that with others. Still others have gotten in the trenches with individual advisors and worked on their behalf to transform their practices, forming a storehouse of case studies with their results.

Well, what if you did all of the above and focused on distilling this activity and experience into a marketing system for financial advisors? That's what you will find here.

> We thank the financial advisors we have worked with for investing their hearts in making a difference in their clients' lives and for dreaming about their own future. We are grateful for their readiness to try out the principles, strategies, and tactics that you will discover in this book.

We chose stories that would demonstrate that you don't need any special advantage to take your practice to the next level. Through their examples, our clients encourage you to break out into new areas of growth. We have changed their names to respect our clients' privacy.

Planning to Boost Production—Emily's Story

As a client, Emily came to us with an underlying grasp of what she'd like her financial advisory practice to be. Yet her focus and her actions were scattered.

Our job was to listen so that we could pick out the threads of her desire for her practice. Then we helped her weave those strands into the special experience she wanted to create for clients and prospects.

Now Emily's Story In Her Words

The Problem: "Developing my marketing was a big task, and sometimes it seemed overwhelming. All these ideas were swimming around, and I didn't know whether they were good and worth pursuing or a waste of time.

"I just reacted to ideas without having any clear direction."

The Action Taken: "Sometimes I felt that what I did was no different from every other financial advisor. Then I began to work with the Hansons. They helped me pull the pieces together and gain real differentiation. Now my unique positioning is generating true excitement."

The Payoff: "Equally important, having my differentiation gives me clarity. The marketing ideas that weren't worthwhile just fell away. Now I have a focused system, *and my production is up a bunch in only a few months!*"

Producing Powerful *Packaging* for Growth—Jeff's Story

The Problem: Jeff and his partner had a promising practice in a large, competitive city. They wanted to direct their practice away from a heavy reliance on insurance to gain a majority of their work from financial planning (both have CFP® certification along with other credentials). While they had deep experience in their field along with years of visibility in their community and they went to extraordinary lengths for their clients, they weren't sure how to create a motivating message.

The Action Taken: We recommended generating their growth foundation first: identifying their target audience and refining their differentiation before creating their communications. Then they focused on packaging their practice (communicating their unique story) with a capabilities deck, a custom website, and a brochure.

The Payoff: Here's how Jeff summed up the outcome of building their growth foundation and creating the packaging that followed. *"Our assets have doubled in 2.5 years*, and much of the growth can be attributed to help from Shirley Hanson and Hanson Marketing in packaging our offering and clarifying who we are. Without the marketing language and materials that she has created, we would not have achieved so much."

Promoting to Attract a Stream of Qualified Prospects Eager to Meet with Him—Ron's Story

The Problem: Ron saw a surge in prospects asking for retirement planning, and he wanted to build on this source of growth.

The Action Taken: We helped Ron position his practice as a retirement planning specialist through a focused website that became the hub of his promotions. Through one marketing campaign, he provided twenty-five retirement tips one-by-one on a popular TV channel. At the same time, he prominently promoted a free retirement planning report throughout the firm's website. He directed prospects to the website through an ad in the city business newspaper. And he increased website traffic through 99 hard-hitting words in a 30-second radio ad during morning drive time.

The Payoff: In the few years since we began to work with him, assets under management went up 50 percent and income increased 67 percent.

Go ahead and set off on your path to your breakthrough. We are by your side as you progress through the sections of the book.

Marketing Power
Your Fast STARt
Break Out of Your Status Quo
7 Steps of Planning
Your Growth Groove
Packaging to Communicate Your Story
Promoting with Systems and Tools

Chapter 2

A Fast STARt out of the STARting Gate

We emphasized the word *STAR* in the title of this chapter because that's what we want for you: to shine as a brilliant star—a *somebody,* a leading light, a luminary—not to languish as a bit player in a crowded field.

"We write this book to inspire you and enable you to achieve your desires for your financial advisory practice and for yourself."
—Bob Hanson and Shirley Hanson

Here's how we intend to do just that ...

We ask you to bring one quality—and only one—to this book. That quality is your desire for a more rewarding and fulfilling practice. Then we will walk by your side to help you have that practice through what you discover in this book.

Simply put, with our belief in your ability and with the client-attraction principles, plans, and practical tools that you'll see in this book, take to heart, and try out, you will succeed.

How You Can Fortify Yourself and Your Practice for Your Breakthrough

You may be a new advisor with no real marketing plan and a practice that is growing through your natural network and sales talent. You may be in mid-career with one or two marketing tactics you've stumbled onto that you are counting on to build your client base. Or you may be an experienced advisor looking for a focused growth plan to add more ideal clients for a more rewarding practice.

Here we give you five mental and emotional "supplements." No matter where you are in the growth of your practice, they can help you get unstuck from your status quo and move with energy and delight toward your desired practice.

1 - Aim as High as You Desire

"The greatest danger in the world for most of us is not that our aim is too high and we miss it, but that it is too low and we reach it."
—Michelangelo

Your Remedy for Results: Instead of being content to accept the business that comes to you, you can take purposeful, positive, and planned steps to attract the business that you truly want.

2 - Be Open-Minded

"They say it can't be done, but that don't always work."
—Casey Stengel

Your Antidote for Relief: A receptive and welcoming mind is fundamental to your success. Don't follow the herd, but be alert to client-attracting ideas from businesses both inside and outside the field of financial services. There's a refreshing torrent of inspiration out there.

3 - Inoculate Yourself against the Deadliest Sin of All—Being Boring

> "Few are those who see with their own eyes
> and feel with their own hearts."
> —Albert Einstein

> "Be your awesome self first, a professional second."
> —Shirley Hanson

It's easy to fall into the dull, predictable "professionalese" trap. When you meet with clients and prospects, you may be able to engage them in a warm conversation. But you may suffer from "professionalization" when you write. It turns up all too often in a financial advisor's biography— an alphabet soup of credentials beside your name, often a list of licenses, and your education with dates.

Relax. There's only one of you, so why sound or act like everyone else?

Your Escape from "Professionalese:" Instead of being remote and all-knowing, add a personal touch that can come only from you. Express a genuine heart-to-heart message from one sincere person to another unique individual.

4 - Discover Those "Magic Words"

> "Everyone has an invisible sign hanging from their neck saying,
> 'Make me feel important.'
> Never forget this message when working with people."
> —Mary Kay Ash

You have seen brochures and websites that are egocentric, talking at the audience with phrases such as "we can offer," "our aim is to," and "we continue to." They selfishly center on a business and its name.

Your Motto for a Better Response: Switch your message to focus on your audience—their pain, their pleasure, and their dreams. Try this: count words like "we," "our," and "us" in your message. Those are the words that promote you and what you are selling. Next, switch your message to focus on your audience. Then it becomes a question of simple arithmetic. Make sure words like "you" and "your" outnumber words that come from your ego.

5 - Release Time

> "Time is the scarcest resource, and unless it is
> managed nothing else can be managed."
> —Peter Drucker

Shirley's Answer: Pearl Bailey just might have been onto something when she said:

"What the world really needs is more love and less paperwork."

Paperwork could be the busywork that gnaws away at our days. It could be the swelling tsunami of information that baffles us or the expectations of instant responses from e-mail and text messages.

Love could be respecting yourself enough to set aside time, perhaps an hour every morning, an afternoon a week, or even a day a week to engage in actions that will unlock your desires for your practice.

Bob's Add-On: Let's get practical. Where can you find time?

> "You will never find time for anything. If
> you want time, you must make it."
> —Charles Buxton

You can make time by eliminating time wasters from your practice. Here we suggest five places to discover time wasters and unlock time for marketing and the growth of your practice.

1 - Look at well-defined processes such as sales, onboarding, client management, and client delivery.

> Where can you streamline your processes for the same or better results? Where can you call on your team to take on some of the routine work you now handle?

2 - Stop marketing and sales tactics that consume time and resources, yet yield little in return.

> Common examples are cold calling and random networking. Switching to "warm" calling and strategic networking or other strategies with a higher ROI will be a better investment of your time.

3 - Face the issue of unprofitable or problem clients.

> Statistically, the bottom 20 percent of your clients are likely to be unprofitable, and at a minimum, never make you any real money. In addition, as many as one in five clients will smother your day with their individual issues that need attention. Cutting back on problem and/or unprofitable clients can not only free as much as a day a week of your time, but also liberate you to slot in a system to add new "A" clients. For example, an independent practice with a normal distribution of 100 clients could roughly double profits/income in less than two years by adding an "A" client per month and handing off one of the bottom 20 percent every month to another advisor.

4 - Reduce the number of quarterly individual meetings with "C" clients.

Let's say you have 70 "C" clients who have been with you for many years, will likely never leave you, don't give you any referrals, and have 100 percent of their assets with you. Spending a total of a day of time on each one per year likely offers minimal to no benefit. Because quarterly meetings were your custom in the past is no reason to perpetuate them.

Suppose you cut back to two meetings a year. Or how about initiating a quarterly conference call, webinar, or workshop with all of them (meeting with them in clusters) and managing the exceptions with individual meetings? Then you could save possibly hundreds of hours per year with potentially *better* results.

5 - Consider not conducting all initial sales meetings face-to-face.

This practice not only can take up to half a day (depending on travel, meeting time, prep time, etc.), but also can reduce the number of prospects you are able to meet with. Charles switched to web meetings as the standard initial step, got 33 percent more potential prospects to take him up on the initial meeting, saved two hours of time on each meeting, and in his case saw no change in his sales conversion.

Whatever steps you take to "make" time, you will have more time to invest productively in growing your practice.

We value your time. Although we've been writing about the strategies, tools, and ideas you'll find here since 1991, we have been ruthless as we prepared this book, throwing out everything but the basics to give you what you need just as you need it. We also will be handing you checklists that give you swift direction and quick guidance on key tools.

You will find them at http://www.marketingplanfinancialadvisor.com/bookresources.html

Now you are ready for your time-tested strategies and tools for your breakthrough.

| Strengthen Your Strengths |
| Break Out Of Your Status Quo |
| Sidestep Pitfalls |
| Energize With Principles |

Chapter 3

How You Can Break Out of Your Status Quo

What Does Your Breakthrough Mean to You?

- ✓ You are frustrated by being stuck on a plateau and would like to increase revenues and assets under management,
- ✓ You are lumped in with the crowd of advisors in your area and want to break out from the pack,
- ✓ You desire to ditch the duds and attract more of the prospects you truly want to work with,
- ✓ You have only a few hours a week for sales and marketing, and you don't want to spin your wheels and waste time,
- ✓ You have several marketing ideas you are considering, but are unsure which ones are right for you,
- ✓ You are looking for a smart strategy to generate a steady flow of referrals from existing and new centers of influence, or
- ✓ You see a special opportunity and want to leverage it for all it's worth.

Call on Your Strengths and Strengthen Your Strengths

"We all have the potential for great accomplishments.
But it's easy to be blindsided by perceptions of your limitations."
—James Owen

The one and only place to start is with you. Instead of being thwarted by thoughts of not being good enough or trying unsuccessfully to fix your weaknesses, begin with what you do well. That's your emotional foundation. And that's how you'll inject real power into your marketing strategies and tactics.

Randy was *very good* at connecting with pre-retiree couples and building a retirement income plan for them. But he was limited by the time available to attract them because he devoted two days a week actively managing his clients' money. Then he found a firm with a 20-year track record with his investment philosophy, and he outsourced his investment management to them. This freed nearly half of his week, which he then focused on a marketing and sales system to take his practice to the next level.

With multiple marketing tactics in place, the new target clients started flowing into his practice. The outcome? Within 18 months, Randy nearly doubled assets under management.

The overriding message in Don Clifton and Paula Nelson's book *Soar with Your Strengths* is "focus on strengths and manage the weaknesses." How this plays out is demonstrated in their book by the answer to a reporter's question to the coach of the Chinese table tennis team about the team's training. The coach's answer: "We practice eight hours a day perfecting our strengths. Here is our philosophy: If you develop your strengths to the maximum, the strength becomes so great it overwhelms the weaknesses"(Clifton and Nelson 1992 and 2010, 19).

Why do you do what you do? The answer becomes your personal mission statement, clarifying your purpose. We've never seen a better explanation of the vital role of mission than this saying by Bill Cosby: "Anyone can dabble, but once you've made that commitment, your blood has that particular thing in it, and it's very hard for people to stop you."

A client came to financial advising after four years as a pastor and 12 years as a high school teacher. He and his family survived the loss of their daughter when she was a senior. He felt "the overwhelming sense of grief that arises when a family member dies and learned how to keep life moving forward while allowing the grieving process to unfold naturally." His mission is "to help people through life's biggest issues."

How Christopher Columbus Strengthened His Strengths

For seven years Columbus tried to persuade the governments of Spain, Portugal, Venice, and Genoa to support his "foolish" scheme to sail west to reach Asia. To them, he held out the vision of discovering a new world along the way.

Through those tough seven years, Columbus honed his strengths.

A big one was his power of persuasion. The son of a weaver and not well-educated, the language barrier could have defeated him. To get a serious hearing, he needed to be able to speak the language of the educated upper classes at the royal courts.

Columbus realized that he had little chance of success unless he could relate to his audience in every possible way. He went way beyond just learning their languages; he took on their dialects.

According to Michael Gelb, who chronicles Columbus's story in *Discover Your Genius*, he absorbed the manners and body language of a courtier. Then he flooded them with the most convincing arguments he could muster (Gelb 2002, 88-113).

Another strength was what's been called his "irrational optimism." Refusing to take no for a answer, he found ways to continue to engage the royal courts. The payoff? As you know, Spain agreed to fund Columbus's voyage.

"The belief in a thing makes it happen."
—Frank Lloyd Wright

You can gain an edge to igniting your breakthrough by avoiding four common marketing stumbles.

Chapter 4

Sidestep These Four Marketing Pitfalls and Potholes on the Path to Your Breakout

Misstep #1 - Betting on One Marketing Technique and One Marketing Technique Only to Carry Your Marketing

Mark, a financial advisor, relied on a nurture system to keep in touch with prospects. We called it his Contact for Life system.

Religiously, he put his newsletter in front of his prospects at least once a month until they asked to be taken off the list or died. That was well and good as far as it went, but it didn't proactively build the business he dreamed of. Counting on one marketing tool for your breakthrough is risky even if it looks like a magic bullet.

Remember, integrating marketing tools can increase their power. A common example today is combining a website (possibly a landing page) with e-mail and a print or pay-per-click ad.

Misstep #2 - Being Mesmerized by the Latest Magic Bullet (or Shiny New Object)

Personally, we'd love to be able to count on one super-duper marketing tool that adds ideal prospects all the time. That won't happen.

Every five years it seems there is a new channel or medium that promises to be the magic elixir, a perpetual prospect gold mine for advisors. Today that magic bullet could be social media. The dream goes something like this: sign up for Twitter, get on Facebook, upload a video to YouTube, create a killer profile for LinkedIn, or start a blog; then watch qualified prospects find you and contact you.

> "Keep in mind that social media is still *media*, and
> before creating your social media strategy,
> it helps to have an overall marketing strategy and media plan.
> Otherwise, any advantage you do gain will be fleeting."
> —Bob Hanson

The "2013 Social Media Marketing Industry Report" by *Social Media Examiner* from a survey of 3000 marketers presents real results. Those marketers found that social media takes time, and by time they point to several hours per week over a three-year commitment. You can't set it once and forget it because it demands long-term allegiance.

Misstep #3 - Counting on Branding as Your Main Marketing Tactic

Branding, according to the American Marketing Association, aims to create "a customer experience represented by a collection of images and ideas; often, it refers to a symbol such as a name, logo, slogan, and design scheme." You will stunt your growth if you count on your logo and a design scheme to dazzle your audience into action. You will fall short of your vision for your practice if you expect a collection of images and a slogan to answer that vital prospect question: why should I choose you over every other financial advisor?

Agonizing over your color scheme and creating the perfect logo can distract you from the real business of marketing. The principles that follow and the 3 P's will enable you to take advantage of the big opportunities in front of you.

Misstep #4 - Feeling Trapped in a Marketing Straitjacket

This marketing stumble can take many forms. It can occur when the last marketing program you devoted more than a year to implement didn't pan out. It can arise when you are stymied and don't know what to do next. It can trap you with the belief that you can't get any business from centers of influence.

One of Houdini's widely popular stunts was to be strapped into a regulation straitjacket and suspended by his ankles from a tall building. Then he flung himself into the air and escaped from the straitjacket in full view of the crowd below.

You don't have to be an escapologist like Houdini to get out of a marketing straitjacket. Timeless, time-tested marketing principles will do the trick. Time is critical for you, as it was for Houdini, so the principles that follow reveal where to put your energy. And even how to snatch success from your marketing duds.

Chapter 5

Marketing Principles to Strengthen You and Motivate You for Your Breakthrough

"Stand for something and you'll never stand alone."
—Gary Bencivenga

In his newsletter the great copywriter Gary Bencivenga revealed his core beliefs as they applied to his specialty of direct response advertising.

"Indeed," he wrote, "standing for something special in your overcrowded marketplace sets you apart from armies of me-too competitors."

In the article "Building Your Company's Vision" in the *Harvard Business Review,* James C. Collins and Jerry I. Porras wrote about the vital role of "fundamental and deeply held core values." They state, "Companies that enjoy enduring success have core values that remain fixed while their business strategies and practices endlessly adapt to a changing world" (Collins and Porras, September 1996).

Their examples include Hewlett-Packard, Procter & Gamble, Nordstrom, and 3M. Think of the McKnight Principles at 3M, such as "Management that is destructively critical when mistakes are made kills initiative. It's essential that we have many people with initiative if we are to continue to grow."

Bob Hanson and Shirley Hanson

Principles Energizing Financial Advisor Practices

As examples, we hand you a few of the principles that are growing advisory practices:

> We believe in integrating your financial life with the rest of your life.

> We believe it is vital for you to understand what you own and why you own it.

> We believe in direct, truthful, and transparent communication with our clients.

> A good plan today is better than a perfect plan tomorrow.

> At the heart of our practice is making a positive difference in our clients' lives.

> We believe in the value of a continuing financial education.

Others are:

> We start with listening: Whatever you can dream, we will put on paper and see how we can help you achieve your dreams.

> First and foremost, we never hold back when it comes to helping you plan for the life you desire. There is so little customer satisfaction today. We intend to supply the difference.

> Many advisors can help you manage your money. We believe in also helping you manage having money. What's the difference? You are no longer hurt by a piecemeal and fragmented approach to your investments.

24

What are your core values? How have you expressed them in your communications? You'll stand out by standing for something. Also, your principles will propel you and your team forward through change and unstable times.

What Are the Core Values Guiding Our Writing?

We believe in you. We appreciate your desire for a more rewarding and fulfilling practice, and we believe in your capacity to achieve your desired practice.

We believe in strengthening your strengths and not dwelling on where you might have fallen short in the past.

We believe in the time-tested strategies, plans, and practical marketing tools that you'll see here, and we will walk by your side to help you flourish.

Rev Up Your Marketing with the 80/20 Principle

The principle of 80/20 marketing is about setting priorities and acting on them.

Alex, who had been in business only a few years, recognized that medical doctors were his firm's "A" clients. We worked with him on a few specific strategies to get in front of small practices. Within a short period of time, he added four doctors in the same month—his best month ever. This never would have happened without 80/20 vision.

For us, 80/20 marketing means "doing the right things and doing things right."

Pareto didn't say it quite that way when he discovered his law and demonstrated it with a mathematical formula. His formula described a recurring pattern in society: some 20 percent of inputs (sometimes called the "vital few") produce about 80 percent of results.

Richard Koch reveals in his book *The 80/20 Principle: The Secret To Success By Achieving More With Less*:

> The few things that work fantastically well should be identified, cultivated, nurtured, and multiplied. At the same time, the waste—the majority of things that will always prove to be of low value to man and beast—should be abandoned or severely cut back (Koch 1998, 20).

Goethe's perspective: Things which matter most must never be at the mercy of things which matter least.

Our Add-On: That's where you have marketing leverage ... by "nurturing" and "multiplying" the marketing principles that can propel your practice to the next level. The next chapter, "P Is for Planning—Seven Steps," gives you a process.

Think Like a Billionaire

That advice comes from master business builder the late Chet Holmes. Wring every ounce of marketing power from your marketing resources. Concentrate your resources (your time, money, and people) on those things that will make the most difference in getting the results you want.

Donald Trump on *The Apprentice* said it another way: "Go big or go home!" As a professional, do you reach high enough? Or do you stay home?

> *It is not the financial advisory practice with the most marketing resources that produces the most leads, but rather it is what a*

practice does with its given marketing resources. The right strategy for you—tested and honed—can beat slick, glitzy, and expensive time after time.

Call on the Five R's to Get the Results You Want

A true story, with help from Alan Greenspan, goes this way: Young artist Erin Crowe, almost fresh out of college, wanted to make money to travel to Europe.

She painted 18 expressionist oil portraits of Alan Greenspan and sold all 18 for as much as $4,000 for one. They sold from the Gallery in Sag Harbor on Long Island, New York. Major Wall Street and hedge fund players vacation there, and they snapped up her paintings.

Why was she so successful? She nailed the five R's of productive results-driven marketing:

1 - Start with the Right People (your ideal prospects)

Erin Crowe's were the Wall Street players who benefited from the Greenspan era from 1987 through 2006.

2 - Craft the Right Message (to reach their hearts and minds)

In Erin's case it was the oil portraits of a dominating figure (Alan Greenspan) for their homes or offices.

3 - Call on the Right Medium

The right medium for her was the art gallery in Sag Harbor, where she easily caught the attention of the prosperous Wall Street crowd on vacation, when they had time to browse and shop.

4 - Act at the Right Time

Just before Alan Greenspan's retirement, when he was incessantly in the news, was the right time for Erin. The right time also included leisure vacation time for her target buyers.

5 - Attract the Right (your desired) Response

She sold all her paintings for enough money for a long, even luxurious, vacation in Europe.

See these five R's for what they are: a proven strategy (tested over more than one hundred years by direct marketers) to deliver the outcome you're after.

This strategy is incorporated into our growth system, which centers on the three P's. Next we unravel each one and give you the strategies and tools you'll need to unlock the potential of your practice.

Connecting the Three P's of Marketing: Easy as 1, 2, 3

When we speak at live or virtual conferences, we try to ask who has incorporated these three P's into their practice. Usually only about 5 percent of advisors have, but these 5 percent invariably correlate to the ones that are growing and thriving.

For a practice to experience sustainable growth over a period of years, it needs to incorporate each of these three P's into the practice.

P Is for Planning – How to generate your **Marketing *Plan*** to attract a steady stream of qualified prospects.

P Is for Packaging – How to communicate your ***Story*** to grab hold of your desired audience.

P Is for Promoting – How to spread the word about your story through high-gain *Promotions* and tactics to speed progress on your road to greater production.

Now we're ready to explore each one of the P's in turn to ignite your marketing momentum.

To help you to get off to a fast start we organized the book around the 3 P's of *Planning* (and its seven steps), *Packaging* (your core communications that tell your story), and *Promoting* (high-gain marketing tools). The chapters on "Getting Into Your Growth Groove" enable you to build a sound foundation for the growth you are looking for.

Our goal is to unlock the power of marketing leverage through a clear-cut system you can call on again and again.

Chapter 6

P Is for Planning—Seven Steps

"If you don't know where you are going,
you might wind up someplace else."
—Yogi Berra

Like Miracle Gro for your financial advisory practice, a marketing plan done right creates "big beautiful results." And a sound plan can generate these results while saving your limited resources of time, money, and people because it eliminates the frustrations of hit-or-miss, haphazard marketing.

7 Steps of Planning
Objectives & Goals
Your Audience
Differentiation
Trust & Believability
Engine for Growth
Reach Prospects
Run the Numbers

Here we put in your hands Seven Steps to a Winning Marketing Plan for Financial Advisors. They are:

Step #1 - Generate Objectives and Goals for Your Marketing Plan that Will Boost Your Chances of Accomplishing Your Business Goals

Step #2 - Target Your Market—Including Zooming In on Their Emotions

Step #3 - Express Your Differentiation through Your Unique Story

Step #4 - Build Trust and Boost Believability

Step #5 - Assemble Your Engine for Growth with Your Marketing Programs, Activities, and Tactics

Step #6 - Reach Your Prospects through Your Media Choices, Lists, Referrals, Co-Marketers, and others

Step #7 - Run the Numbers—Budget, Leads, and Timing, Along with Cost-Per-Client and Return on Investment

Your marketing plan can guide you to put your best foot forward, catapult your financial advisory practice above a crowded field of competitors, generate new clients and referrals, and nurture current clients to become better ones.

Or it can be a wasted opportunity and a source of frustration. From time to time, Bob has worked with wirehouse management and advisors. There he saw that thousands of advisors were required to create marketing or business plans, and they spent many hours researching and crafting them. Almost to each advisor, their carefully considered plans were not implemented but were left on a shelf and ignored. That's why it's vital to plan the details of action—exactly who will do what, when, where, and how. Consider your plan as a simple, straightforward road map to follow to your desired destination.

Your Seven Steps to a Winning Marketing Plan for Financial Advisors

> "By failing to prepare, you are preparing to fail."
> —Benjamin Franklin

This seven-point plan hands you proven strategies plus tips, tools, and tactics to transform your new marketing plan—or an existing plan—into your road map for more effective marketing, for greater production, for more and better clients, and for more fun.

Step #1 - Generate Objectives and Goals for Your Marketing Plan that Will Boost Your Chances of Accomplishing Your Business Goals

The more concrete your objectives for the marketing plan, the better you can measure them, and the more likely you are to achieve them. A marketing plan should support your practice goals or overall business plan, whether that plan is formal or informal.

Also, here you will clarify your specific marketing objectives. These could be, for instance, setting up for each month five first appointments with new prospects who have a specific retirement issue. Or they could be communicating with clients quarterly about the range of services you offer to prompt a total of $1 million in new assets under management from clients during each quarter. You could decide as an objective to add five more referrals each month or to activate one marketing event each quarter through complementary partners.

Questions to answer include:

> Q - What are my specific goals for fees or income?
>
> Q - What are the types of new clients I would like to acquire?
>
> Q - How much business will come from different sources (existing clients/new clients)?
>
> Q - How will I know my marketing plan is successful during the time period of the plan?

Step #2 - Target Your Market—Including Zooming In on Their Emotions

Financial prospects, like other buyers, *buy emotionally and justify their decisions with facts and logic.* While it is excellent to have all sorts of quantitative data about your target market, both on average and as a group, make sure you are able to address their emotional problems—ones you can solve.

Questions to answer include:

> Q - Who is my target market(s) in as much detail as possible?
>
> Q - What are the major financial problems and emotional pain points that I can help to resolve?
>
> Q - If I have more than one target market, what priority do I assign to each one?

This step leads to your ideal client discovery, which strengthens your growth foundation. (See your step-by-step guide in the next chapter, "Getting into Your Growth Groove: Ideal Client Discovery.") You will discover how to grow your business by knowing with certainty *what your prospects and clients want from you.* That's vital information to help you:

- Develop profitable positioning,
- Attract qualified higher net worth prospects,

- Multiply referrals, and
- Convert prospects to clients with the right message.

Step #3 - Express Your Differentiation through Your Unique Story

What's your story and how are you uniquely positioned to serve your target market? Many marketing plans fail to put life into the financial advisor's story. As a result, prospects (and also clients) don't get a sense of who *you are or how you are different.* You have missed a golden opportunity to connect with another individual and nudge a prospect closer to being a client.

Ideally, you will have a large and spacious version of your differences, with key building blocks that communicate why you are in a category of one and, in addition, a short capsule statement such as a tagline.

Questions to answer here include:

Q - What is my unique story?
Q - What are my personal strengths in working with clients?
Q - What is my process for engaging clients and making them successful over the long term?
Q - What key investment services do I offer?
Q - What is my investment philosophy?
Q - How can I express my differentiation in words?

Do *not* expect your prospects and clients to do the hard work of figuring out what your financial-advising practice is all about. Chapter 8, "Getting into Your Growth Groove: How You Can Leave the Pack Behind," will accelerate your path to a category of one.

Step #4 - Build Trust and Boost Believability

Your job is to relieve your prospects' doubts. To do this requires both credibility and believability. Credibility comes from your credentials and qualifications. But credibility will take you only so far.

Believability comes from *proof.*

At the bottom of the 2013 Harris Interactive USA Summary Report on its Reputation Quotient survey, you will find the category "Tobacco," and above it, "Government." Go up one more category and you will see "Banking" and then "Financial Services." Above "Financial Services" are 11 categories with higher industry reputation ratings.

To separate yourself from the scoundrels and wrongdoers, ask these questions:

> Q - How can I communicate and validate that I am worthy of trust?
> Q - How and when can I talk about fees to allay concerns?
> Q - What steps can I take to demonstrate that I keep commitments?

Chapter 9, "Getting into Your Growth Groove: How You Can Nail These Eight Faces of Trust and Believability," will enable you to stand out as worthy of trust.

Step #5 - Assemble Your Engine for Growth with Your Marketing Programs, Activities, and Tactics

These are the programs, tactics, and activities that will deliver your marketing message over the period of the plan.

Caution: Avoid a one-legged marketing plan by embracing more than one way of generating new prospects each and every month. Also consider: you can have a separate set of tactics for clients, for centers of influence, and for prospects.

Examples of common tactics include seminars, webinars or presentation recordings, direct mail, newsletters or white papers/free reports, columns in newspapers, personal networking or use of social media networking such as LinkedIn, talks to groups or associations, online ads, event or organization sponsorships, magazine ads, meeting campaigns, and numerous others. An ongoing referral strategy may be a key activity of your plan.

Initially, your prime task is to develop a list of tactics with which you can be successful—both in building from your strengths and in reaching your target market. As you finalize the plan, this list can feed into a marketing calendar, which shows when and how you will implement your selected tactics.

Questions to answer in this section of the plan include:

> Q - What are the key programs or tactics that I can call on to attract leads and interest?
> Q - Does this list of tactics play to my strengths and also reach the target market?
> Q - Exactly when will these marketing tactics occur?

You will discover more about developing this key in chapters 10 and 11 on Packaging and Promoting.

Step #6 - Reach Your Prospects through Your Media Choices, Lists, Referrals, Co-Marketers, and More

The different media you select can include online and offline publications, direct mail lists, associations or groups, your own list, or lists from other organizations or businesses.

To reach, for instance, 2,000 higher net worth prospects in your area, you may want to consider a combination of direct mail, e-mail, and online ads. Also, recognize that other businesses could have a good list of your target prospects that you may be able to draw on.

Remember: Select your specific, definable target market first, and then look for the most responsive and appropriate media from the range of options.

Questions to answer in this section include:

> Q - Who has a list or publication that reaches my specific target market(s)?
> Q - What media do they consume (TV, radio, social media, lifestyle publications, or others)?
> Q - How can I most effectively reach both prospects and clients to prompt them to respond?

Step #7 - Run the Numbers—Budget, Leads, and Timing, Along with Cost-Per-Client and Return on Investment

Being Strategic Means to Track Results Relentlessly.

While many financial advisors track the overall dollar cost of marketing efforts or of a specific tactic along with the overall number of clients generated from marketing, they rarely go beyond that. You will want to know more.

Like what? Well, like key metrics such as numbers of clients from different sources, cost per lead, cost per client, return on marketing investment, and projected year-one and lifetime value of the client. You may also consider the time required for marketing and selling as a cost and track that, too.

This information will guide you to add, subtract, or fine-tune your marketing strategies and tactics. Without it, you're in the dark. By running the numbers, you will have valuable information about the most profitable way to continue.

Questions to answer in this section include:

> Q - What are the number of leads and clients created from each tactic by month?
>
> Q - What is the cost of an individual program (including the investment of your money, people, and time) and the total costs of specific tactics over time?
>
> Q - Moving forward, which tactics should get less emphasis and which tactics demand more?

It comes down to this: The most profitable marketing plans build on an effective strategy. Being strategic enables you to wring every ounce of marketing power from your marketing resources. Then it's up to you to act on your marketing plan through its multiple actions on multiple fronts to reap your bountiful harvest of clients year after year.

William's Story of Big Payoffs

William is guided by his 12-month marketing calendar, propelled by his purpose to "educate, communicate, and connect" not only with prospects, clients, and influencers but also with his team.

He acts on his belief that "you can't stop getting your name out there." His calendar includes workshops every three months for CPAs and attorneys. Recently, William sat in front of a $120 million prospect, a referral from another advisor who was retiring. Once William's student, the advisor acknowledged that "William taught me everything I know."

Did William gain this ultra high net worth client? No, because the prospect was looking for a firm with multiple partners. William is certain, though, that his growth plan will reap qualified prospects and ideal clients again and again. For example, another student (an accountant) built a practice from what he learned from William years ago. Upon retiring, he turned over his top clients (which totaled $10 million in assets) to William. "We know," William said, "that each tactic we are executing right now will pay off big."

Next, prepare for growth with your growth framework

Your Growth Groove
Ideal Client Discovery
Leave the Pack Behind
8 Faces of Trust

Chapter 7

Getting into Your Growth Groove:
Ideal Client Discovery

The late Gary Halbert said it best:
"Research is a cheap way to make sure you'll hit the right nerve!"

Market intelligence lets you address the issues you uncover to create a profitable marketing system. You will *avoid* the futile, disheartening, and wasteful task of trying to force something on a closed-minded market. And it guides you to the services and products to focus on to become truly extraordinary.

How do you acquire this rock-solid market intelligence? Tune in to the true marketing geniuses: your target audience. Just ask, and then you'll know *without doubt*. Here we outline a practical technique to gain vital intelligence from both prospects and active clients to boost the number of prospects who become clients.

1. *Analyze your current client list* – Practice the 80/20 rule. You are looking for the "vital few," the small percent of clients who produce most of the results.

2. *List all possible market segments you are interested in attracting* – Examples are manufacturing firms in a niche, franchise owners, widows, family-owned businesses, pre-retirees, medical professionals, or perhaps even more specifically anesthesiologists.

These do not have to be currently represented in your book of business.

3. *Assign a priority to each segment,* starting with the segment you most want to attract.

4. *Answer questions for each segment to fill out a preliminary sketch, starting with your number one target market priority.* You can ask a few of your clients in this market segment to answer key "research" questions. Continue with your second-priority target segment.

The types of questions we suggest cover vital statistics and your target audience's psychological traits and emotional states.

Their Vital and Social Statistics (demographics)

Will they likely be able to meet your minimum business requirements?

Their age?

Are they male or female? (Your market segment may include both.)

Where are they located?

What changes will soon occur in their business or their lives (children going off to college, IRA rollover, sale of business, want to grow a business, retirement, etc.)?

Their Psychological Traits (psychographics)

What are their biggest frustrations and complaints in the areas where you provide solutions? List as many pain points as you can that resonate with your target audience. We organize the list under themes and situations such as:

Frustrations with Current Investment Situation

Example: Upset with current investment advisor because of lack of communication

Personal Situation Demands Attention

Example: Worry about having enough money to last through retirement

Fears about Current U.S. or World Economic Situation

Example: Feel overwhelmed by the relentless stream of information and misinformation

Marketer extraordinaire Dan Kennedy in an intense Copywriting Coaching Club that Shirley participated in gave permission to pass along his "smart" research questions. Seek answers to questions such as:

What keeps them awake at night, indigestion boiling up in their esophagus, eyes staring at the ceiling?

What are they afraid of?

What are they angry about—who are they angry at?

What are their top three daily frustrations?

43

What do they secretly, ardently desire most?

What do they desire least?

You may also want to answer these additional questions:

Are they demanding or appreciative of your time and service?

Are they prominent in your community and have contacts to the people you would like to have as clients?

You will see a direct correlation between how well you know and understand the individuals in your target audience and how effectively you will be able to attract more of them ... and convert them to clients.

It's never been easier to gather intelligence. Ask smart questions in a one-on-one survey of your clients. Get feedback from your advisory group or sounding board. (If you don't have one, consider creating one.) For 15 years Rick has called on his sounding board, which meets quarterly, to help his "practice stay focused on what clients want from us."

Other ways to gather intelligence include:

- Answer the question, "Who else knows about the needs and wants of my target audience?" Besides clients it could be, for example, suppliers or sales reps.
- Follow top bloggers who write for your target audience. Note which posts get the most comments.
- Check out top sellers in your field at Amazon.com and pay attention to the bullet-point benefits on the front and back covers.

- Sign up for Google Alerts and get news about your selected topics through e-mail day after day.
- Surf appropriate forums for hot topics. Try asking questions there.

There is no better use of your marketing and prospecting time than gathering intelligence if you truly want to fast-forward to create powerful differentiation and achieve your vision for your business.

Chapter 8

Getting into Your Growth Groove: How You Can Leave the Pack Behind

You may feel as if you are stuck in the jumble of just-like-everyone-else financial advisors. This can happen if you:

- Call on your logo, company name, or a dull, no-guts phrase to convey your uniqueness,
- Rely on a characterless, plain-vanilla, me-too message, or
- Hope glitz and gimmicks in your brochure, website, and other sales materials will dazzle your visitors into action.

What's wrong here? You fail to answer critical questions such as:

- What compelling reasons do prospects have to do business with me?
- What steps can I take now to break away from everyone else in my field?

If you are counting on others to puzzle out the answers for you, you've lost a major competitive edge that could be yours.

Al Ries and Jack Trout in *Positioning: The Battle for Your Mind* expanded on the strategy of differentiating.

> Positioning is what you do to the mind of the prospect. That is you position [your practice] in the mind of the prospect.

Differentiation will enable you to profit from your strengths and your competitors' weaknesses. It will prevent you from making one of the biggest marketing mistakes most financial advisors make: to be ego-centered, not client-focused. And it will keep you from falling into the costly—sometimes fatal—trap of *trying to be all things to all people.*

Without differentiation, your business has a ghostly presence. With it your clients and prospects will grasp at once—dramatically, memorably, and specifically—how you solve their problems.

What Differentiation Is *Not* Is As Revealing As What It *Is*

It's not a smoke-and-mirrors trick to distract people from an ordinary product or service.

It's not a boring, flabby summing-up like this: "We are a global, full-service financial firm, which provides brokerage, investment banking, and asset management services to corporations, governments, and individuals around the world."

It's not a shallow or artificial claim. It must hit the core of your business. It must be in sync with your *mission and vision* for your firm. And you must be able to keep the promises expressed by your positioning.

Most important, it's not about settling for being in a commodity business and believing every financial advisor does pretty much the same thing. And that may be the most *vital change* we are asking of you. *What we reveal is how to make competition irrelevant.*

First, Be Sure Your Practice Is Ready.

Your business must offer first-class products and services.

> Successful marketing of less than grade A products or services could cause a business to falter.

It must deliver what it promises. No question about it!

It must be client centered.

> A common mistake many financial advisors make is to be ego-centered—not to center attention on the client. Their error comes from talking about what interests them or falling back on industry jargon. Your clients are fixated on one thing: the benefits they get from doing business with you. They can be egotistic. That's okay. But if you are self-centered, your practice will suffer.

Good, that's out of the way. Now you are ready for ...

Eight Differentiating Ideas with Rich Potential for Financial Advisors

As a financial advisor, you may find your differentiation in a combination of these eight rewarding ideas (or in ideas that you may add to this list). Business-building consultant Paul Lemberg challenges businesses to find what he calls "Ten Must-Haves." You may not uncover ten differentiating points, but search for as many as possible.

1. Call on Benefits, Benefits, Benefits
2. Find Your Differentiation in Your Target Market
3. Bring Your Specialness to Light
4. Tell the Story Only You Can Tell

5. Capitalize on What Your Competition Can't or Won't Do
6. Do Well by Doing Good
7. Connect Your Name to an Event
8. Name Your System or Process

1. Call on Benefits, Benefits, Benefits

> "Benefits unlock your business success and
> separate you from the me-too pack."
> —Doug Hall

To get started, a simple and productive technique is to divide a piece of paper into two columns. On one side list every fact and feature of your practice.

And on the other side, list every benefit and promise for that feature. Often there will be more than one benefit for each feature or fact.

Facts and Features	Benefits
(examples)	
17 years of experience	You get a proactive process that helps to carry you through the uncertainties of the financial world because I've been tested by the ups and downs of the markets.
	You gain the results you want because you can tap into the team of experts I have assembled during these years.
Limiting my practice to 67 clients	You get a financial advisor who takes time to get to know you and your family and help you create the life you desire.

> I schedule time (as Rick does) to focus with you individually on "areas beyond money—on your physical, mental, and spiritual well-being and on your personal relationships."

You are seeking benefits that matter *hugely* to your prospects. Go with the ones that will inject the greatest energy into your differentiation and will mean the most to your prospects and clients.

2. Find Your Differentiation in Your Target Market

Where's the right target market for you?

- divorced women,
- middle-income individuals facing retirement,
- energy executives,
- top executives in large firms,
- small family-owned businesses,
- Gen X and Gen Y professionals such as attorneys (or a sub-segment such as estate attorneys), dentists, real estate professionals, or others,
- an affinity group such as people associated with a popular and worthwhile charity,
- geography—a few key zip codes (if this is your choice, prepare to dominate your chosen area), or
- is it in another target market?

If you choose a target market, be sure you can answer the smart questions and zoom in on their pain points from your "gathering vital intelligence" work in the previous chapter. Each market has its own needs, frustrations, and opportunities. Each has different expectations.

3. Bring Your Specialness to Light

As Jack Trout said in his book *Trout on Strategy,* "The secret weapon of the specialist is to be perceived as the best, the expert."

Your prospects think of you first. Simply, you become the only choice. Where can you look for your specialness? It can exist in *your target market.* Or you can *tie your specialness to a particular process, service, or solution.*

Your specialness can be *in giving extraordinary service.* Warning: If you choose this area, you really must wow prospects and clients with their experience of working with you. Not only that, but everyone on your team must be on board to provide this same high-voltage service.

People's expectations are higher than ever. Good isn't nearly good enough. Remember, your competition is not only the firms in your field that provide first-rate service, but businesses in every field. Your prospects will compare you to *everyone else!*

4. Tell the Story Only You Can Tell

> "There is no subject or personality in the world that doesn't have some kind of twist that will interest people.
> You will find it if you look."
> —Copywriter John Carlton

Don't discount your personal story. It may generate the right words to distinguish you.

You may find it in your stellar skills, your upbringing, your heritage, your special personality, or your interests and passions. You may discover it in the things that are easiest for you. Or it may be in your business or personal experiences.

- What are the two greatest gifts you received as a child?
- What's important to you?
- What are you proud of?
- What propelled you into the business of being a financial advisor?
- Where is the human interest in your story?

We uncovered this story by asking John, "Why did you become a financial advisor?"

> By the time I was 13, I had saved $36,000 from my lawn boy business. I earned it the hard way at $12 per lawn. I hadn't a clue about how to keep my money safe and also open the door for growth. One thing I was sure of, I didn't want to go backward and lose money.

> Finding answers became my lifetime quest for myself, and later for my clients.

Another place to discover your company story is your history. If you choose this one, blend the old with your current efforts to keep up-to-date.

5. Capitalize on What Your Competition Can't or Won't Do

Your prospects may believe you are pretty much the same as other businesses in your field ... until you show them that you are demonstrably different. Where does your competition fall short?

- Do you have special information that they don't?
- Do you have a skill they don't possess?
- Can you provide a service your competition can't or won't?

Leverage this information for your own differentiation. Expose big problems that matter. Disclose your solution.

It comes down to this: Don't go head-to-head where your competitors are strong. Leapfrog ahead on their weaknesses. Perhaps the weakness you see is being a generalist—trying to be all things to all people. As Jack Trout said in *Trout on Strategy*:

> People tend to be impressed with those who focus on a specific activity or product. They are seen as experts in the field and may be given more credit than their experience or knowledge merit. *Generalists, on the other hand, are rarely given credit for their expertise in a number of areas.* [The emphasis is ours.]

Discover a way to tie into your own unique strengths and become a clear winner!

6. Do Well by Doing Good

Your connection to a charity can create a fascinating story. Pick an issue that's important to your target audience and meaningful to you—where your heart is. And find a way to affiliate with this group in a powerful way.

Emily targeted women as her most desired clients, and her charity work centered on women's issues. She stood out by rolling up her shirtsleeves to chair a committee for a foundation that provides money to help improve women's lives.

Ryan, a CFP® and also a CPA, chaired a committee for his local CPA association that awards scholarships to local students. As spokesperson, his committee work gave him positive press coverage.

Paul especially loves working with children and seeing tangible evidence of making a difference. He wants to help enhance their lives "by providing something they may not see otherwise." To accomplish this mission he became an officer on a foundation board and chaired its mud volleyball tournament, which has grown from grossing $200,000 to become one of the largest fund-raisers in the state.

By connecting deeply and genuinely with a charity, you generate affinity with other caring people.

7. Connect Your Name to an Event

How To: The secret to making an event produce clients is to start with the end in mind. What do you want to be different after the event? Then the next question to ask is, "How will this event do that for me?" If you can't answer that question, then it's a waste of your marketing resources to continue.

How Not To: Sam sponsored a popular, exclusive golf event for low-handicap golfers who wanted to become even better. To help them, Sam flew in a specialist to show them how to beat their best score.

In his case, he wanted to attract three or four ideal clients from the event. This never happened because he didn't choreograph the event to give him what he wanted. The golfers outdid their previous low scores, his strategic partners benefited, and the golf specialist was well paid for the outing (and even attracted new business). Sam's (largely anonymous) role was to pay the bills.

We worked with Sam on identifying the people he wanted to attend and then taking steps to make sure they were invited. It sounds elementary, but in the past it was left to chance. Another step was to ensure that he got the credit by being visible throughout. It didn't pay to be a behind-the-scenes, hidden benefactor.

8. Name Your System or Process

Naming your system or process can engage your prospect's imagination and highlight your ability. It enables your prospects to grasp your benefits immediately. What's more, it can grab and keep your prospects' attention.

A financial advisor has his "Four-Step Realization Process." Another has his "Five C's Wealth Management Process." Another has his "Six Pillars," and he has been very successful with his custom monthly newsletters with their variations on one or more of these pillars.

Next, Blend or Fuse Your Positioning Points to Build Your Strongest Case

Michael does this extraordinarily well. He asks two questions. First he asks, "Why do clients choose to work with us?" Then he offers nine reasons, including his core values, his business beliefs, his planning process, his mission, and his services.

His second question, "What makes us different?" opens the door to six more differentiators, such as how we manage risk, investment philosophy, how we are compensated, and giving back. Giving back isn't a list of the boards and charities he is connected with. Instead, he presents benefits such as "enhancing the community" or "inspiring young people to service." With each one, he reveals exactly how he works to accomplish this advantage.

Your differentiation is a memorable, persuasive, and motivating summing-up that zooms in on your strengths and the strengths of your practice. You can start with a few, as Michael did, and add to your differentiation year after year. Be sure to promote your message like crazy.

The Payoff for You: Your marketing will become more fun as your voice soars above the clatter and high-quality prospects gravitate to you.

Chapter 9

Getting into Your Growth Groove: How You Can Nail These Eight Faces of Trust and Believability

You may feel as if you are hamstrung by relentless reports of greed, misdeeds, and billion-dollar fines and penalties. Besides, the stigma persists that advisors are pushers of products and services and that they treat clients like "muppets" (idiots).

> "We can increase trust—much faster than we might think—
> and doing so will have a huge impact,
> both in the quality of our lives and in the
> results we're able to achieve."
> —Stephen M. R. Covey in *The Speed of Trust (Covey 2008, 3)*

What can you do to dispel skepticism, mistrust, and doubt and bridge the credibility gap? These "Eight Faces of Trust and Believability" show you how.

1. Prove That You and Your Clients Are on the Same Side of the Table

That's easy to say, but where's the proof? William, a top advisor in the United States, handles it with a reassuring message: he lets prospects know (and reminds clients) about how he "controls and minimizes investment costs. There are fees that clients aren't aware of," he explains. "If we screen right, we can squeeze these out."

2. Keep Commitments to Yourself and to Your Clients

Matt was described in his survey of his clients with the heartwarming phrase, "Trust with a Capital T." Stephen M. R. Covey may have explained why Matt won such a powerful feeling of trust when he wrote, "One of the fastest ways to [build] and restore trust is to make and keep commitments—even very small commitments—to ourselves and others." *(Covey 2008, 13)*

Here's an example of a common situation that you can change. Don't lie about small things, such as having your assistant tell a caller that you are in a meeting when you are not. Matt earned his "Trust with a Capital T" by small daily courtesies and concern for his clients and, also, caring enough to keep his commitments.

3. Demonstrate that You Are Good at What You Do

This is something we insist on in bios, brochures, and websites. If you have credentials, please don't take them for granted. And please don't assume that your prospects understand what they mean.

The initials CFP* are meaningless unless you explain that this certification requires (as of 2013) qualifying experience, rigorous coursework, passing a two-day exam, and adhering to a high standard of ethics in addition to 30-hours of continuing education every two years. What's more, it covers a broad range of planning topics, including investments, insurance, income tax, retirement, and estate planning.

4. Muster Every Ounce of Relevant Experience

Jeff told us this fascinating story. A husband and wife were hunting for a new advisor. In checking out many options in a large, affluent city, they visited Jeff's website.

Here they saw on the home page that the two partners have "more than 60 years of combined financial experience"—both are CFP®s, one has an MBA, the other had been a CPA for 20 years.

So how did this play out? The wife revealed that she wouldn't want to work with any firm that had less than this level of experience. She was sold, and Jeff's firm added another $1.5 million to their assets under management.

5. Follow a Fiduciary Standard

A *fiduciary standard* means that the advisor acts always in the best interest of their clients—they have an obligation to act in a way that best meets each client's needs. For CFP® certification, for example, the advisor follows a fiduciary standard.

6. Take the Mystery out of Your Fees

An enlightening report called "A Matter of Trust" came from the University of Pennsylvania's Wharton School and State Street Global Advisors. This report makes the strongest connection between coming across as trustworthy with being upfront about your fees. And here are three steps to take:

- Talk about fees early in the relationship. You'll allay fears right away and begin to build trust.
- Present a simple, single fee structure.
- Put fees in writing so that prospects don't have to rely on memory. That way, there won't be doubt or confusion later.

Consider revealing your fees on your website. Michael has a special section on his website that asks and answers, "What is our fee structure? How are we compensated?"

7. Become An "Eternal Student"

Luciano Pavarotti, one of the greatest tenors ever, called himself an "eternal student." Being an "eternal student" shows that you are not stuck in the old ways nor left behind in a high-speed world. *It's only on the game shows where there is a "final answer."*

Ray has a passion for research, with seven screens in his office all providing up-to-the-minute information from the top-level services he subscribes to—the same ones that large institutions pay big bucks for. When he recommends something to a client, it's not last-year's answer, but up-to-the-minute results from an exhaustive search through his sources and resources.

8. Give Back

You can inspire and uplift others, and counter mistrust, by revealing your altruistic side.

Martin, a financial advisor, has helped a nonprofit in his city raise over $40,000. He went far beyond sitting on a board or giving a nice contribution. He took on the job of events planner and shouldered all the nitty-gritty details to put on the events. Also, he became the master of ceremonies to stand out as the face of the nonprofit at the events.

With your marketing plan and growth foundation ready for action, we move to the second P, Packaging.

Your Packaging
Your Voice & Personality
Website Must-Haves
Your Winning Pitch
Brochures That Pay Off

Chapter 10

P Is for Packaging

Bob describes packaging as your core communications that tell your story. Shirley's addendum: They tell the story that only you can tell.

Which practice is likely to grow faster, be more profitable, and have greater production? It's the one that specializes and communicates that specialness.

When You Devise Your Communications Strategy, What Will Be Your Personality and Your Voice?

Your strategy should match both your personality and practice and also resonate with your prospects and clients. An active researcher, for example, may do a daily update on the markets. An advisor who has worked in a community for 27 years and heads the foundation for the largest university in the county may weave local news and references into his communications. An advisor building a practice around widows could walk by her audience's side with empathy and advance an educational perspective.

Questions to answer when packaging your practice include:

> Q - What tone will you use when you communicate?
> Q - What themes, financial topics or problems, or life issues will you talk about?

Q - Will you come from the point of view of education, better financial performance, personal improvement, financial planning, commonsense strategies, reading the trends in the markets and the economy, managing individual behavior, problem solving, or something else?

Q - What types of communication vehicles will you use (a pitch book, a brochure, a website, a blog, or another of dozens of media choices)?

What's behind the story that only you can tell?

Your story reveals who you are and how you help others.
It conveys a clear, consistent, coordinated message. It could be as concise as a four-word tagline ("Managing Wealth Made Simple") or as expansive as your website.

At the heart of your story are your unique answers to one key question:

Why should I choose you over every other advisor?

The power of your packaging comes from the strength of your growth foundation: your ideal prospect discovery and your points of differentiation, along with your credibility and believability boosters. There you'll discover a storehouse of ideas, advantages, and words to call on for your communications.

You'll find many facets of differentiation in chapter 8, "Getting into Your Growth Groove: How You Can Leave the Pack Behind." Now we add your Unique Selling Proposition (USP), or what some marketers call your Unique Value Proposition (UVP), a quick solid differentiator to have ready for the right occasions.

Consider calling on major benefits for your USP. Marketer extraordinaire Dan Kennedy suggests ranking your benefits by:

- Their importance to your target audience and
- How much potential they have to differentiate you from your competition.

Another approach to your differentiation is to ask the journalist's who, what, when, where, why, and how questions:

Who is my target audience?

What does my target market want most?

What do they want least?

What is the big problem that I solve that almost no other advisor addresses?

When do they want the solution I can offer?

Where do they want it?

Why do they want it?

How do they want it?

"What do they want least?" is a vital question. For your target audience, for instance, their pain points may be a lack of control over their financial future or the fear of running out of money over a long retirement lasting 25 or more years.

In grad school a professor of Shirley's always asked at the end of what seemed to be a wide-ranging, rambling class discussion, "Who wants to wrap it up and tie a ribbon around it?" So here we show you how to wrap up your message and tie a ribbon around it.

A Small Package: Your Capsule USP (Your Tagline)

The capsule USP (your tagline) could go on your business card, on your stationery, on the banner of your website, and in your signature file in an e-mail. Simply, it must be the right words to grab your ideal prospects' attention and help you stand out from the pack. And if it succeeds, it will be compelling, unique, and memorable for them.

Examples from financial advisors are: "Independent Research Can Make the Difference," "Managing Wealth Made Simple," "Helping You Navigate through Uncertain Waters" (for an advisor on a coastal island), "Helping You Achieve Your Goals for Your Life," and "Aligning the Means and Meaning of Your Life."

A Somewhat Larger Package: Your Elevator (or Waiting-in-the-Takeout-Line) Speech

A financial advisor was waiting in the takeout line to pick up a pizza order. In conversation with the man behind him, the man asked, "What do you do?"

F.A. responded: "I'm a financial advisor."

The Man Waiting in Line: "There are a lot of them around."

Then and there, the financial advisor was dismissed, or rather he set himself up to be dismissed. But suppose he had a short, one sentence takeout-line or elevator speech ready; then he could move the conversation forward. So let's take it from the top.

Person in Line: What do you do?

F.A.: I help those planning for retirement answer their tough question, "Will I be financially okay?"

Then watch for the eyes-light-up reaction. When you sense a response or hear a question that signals, "This is important and I'd like to find out more," you have an invitation to move into your list of must-haves. Select one that follows closely on the elevator speech and expands on anything you may have figured out about the person in line. You could answer by explaining, "You gain a coach in your corner with 24 years of experience helping people reduce stress as they prepare for retirement."

A compelling elevator speech:

> Flags your prospects,
>
> Names their problem, and
>
> Offers a solution, or emotional payoff.

Develop your own statement so that you seize attention and generate interest. The reaction you want is (and this can happen, too, when you're face-to-face with *a qualified prospect*), "Tell me more." You have the opportunity to ask questions, to get details about their situation, and expand the conversation.

A Longer Story When You Have Room to Stretch

In writing (whether your brochure, website, a sales letter, your biography, or in another communication vehicle), your differentiation can be unfolded into a longer story. This story from a financial advisor is not your usual buttoned-down bio. Matt's story begins like this:

"I grew up in a tough inner-city neighborhood in New York. As a young teenager, I looked at my peers and at how people around me were living and said, 'This is not for me. There's a lot more our society has to offer.' Fortunately, I was not alone." *And the story continues.*

Your website hands you the opportunity to tell your full story, and it affords your audience the ability to experience its facets as they like. In today's world, your website can be your 24/7/365 brochure *and* a whole lot more.

Ten Must-Haves for a Website That Wins Clients

Let's separate the designer's version of a website from the marketer's version. The designer's version promotes pretty pictures and design elements first and foremost. Neatly tucked into the design, the words are nice, but bland. They could speak for almost any firm to almost any audience.

The marketer's version of a website gives your carefully selected audience a choice. And what's that choice? Plain and simple, it's a reason to choose you over every other financial advisory practice.

Advisors experience again and again what happened to Jim. Jim had a designer's website for ten years and could not recall a single qualified prospect from his site. Within 90 days of launching his new website with many of the must-haves below, he received a prospect's inquiry from the site that became his biggest client relationship, with $5 million in investable assets.

Here we give you a Ten Must-Haves System for a website that shepherds your prospects and those who know you, such as clients and centers of influence, to "Yes!" "Yes!" for prospects could be to take the next step, for example, to sign up for a white paper written with them in mind. For centers of influence, "Yes!" could be to more fully grasp whom you help and send a referral your way. For clients, "Yes!" could be to fully understand all you do and why, and add more assets under your management.

Must-Have #1 - I am clear about my website's primary purpose.

My website is tightly organized around that purpose (including design, navigation, and links). I can add secondary purposes, but I am careful not to confuse website visitors by bombarding them with too many possibilities or sending them hither and yon.

Must-Have #2 - My website focuses, first and foremost, on very important people (*not* on me and my colleagues)—on my top clients, ideal prospects, and/or key centers of influence.

Must-Have #3 - I have seeded my content broadly and deeply with my differentiation.

It's more than a clever tagline. It displays all facets of why I am in a category of one and how I can help to reduce the pain of my audience(s) and assist them in achieving their desired goals.

Must-Have #4 - My home page radiates marketing magnetism for my chosen audience(s).

It's not a recital of a vague mission statement. Instead, it zooms in on exactly how I can make my clients' and prospects' lives better.

Must-Have #5 - I have created case studies (crafted to meet compliance requirements) for my website so that these stories become lodged in my site visitors' minds.

They know without doubt the key problems I am expert in resolving and for whom, how I go about helping my clients put their worries behind them, and exactly how I remove obstacles so that their lives became easier and happier.

Must-Have #6 - I have incorporated into my website at least five ways to build credibility and believability. (See chapter 9, "Getting into Your Growth Groove: How You Can Nail These Eight Faces of Trust And Believability.")

Now that you have a website chock-full of your most wanted components, you'll want to be sure that it appeals to the search engines. How about search engine optimization? Jill Whalen of High Rankings asserts that instead of focusing on how to make specific keyword phrases rank better in Google, "create a great website that Google will have to show highly because to omit it from their listings would be a great disservice to their searchers."

Be aware that having a productive website is more involved than just getting traffic from the search engines.

Here's How Your Website Can Work for You ...

Must-Have #7 - On every page I call my website visitors to action.

In no uncertain terms, I let them know what I would like them to do next. It could be to download a checklist, report, or white paper. It could be to contact me for a "Wealth Review" or a "Second Opinion." Or it could recommend that they check out my "Case Studies" or prompt them to discover more about my financial planning process for making a difference in the lives of people just like them.

Must-Have #8 - My clients receive kid-glove treatment.

I train them to log in to their accounts through the website. I announce webinars and special events for them and arrange for them to sign up on the website. While they are passing through, I am reinforcing what I do for them, solidifying our relationship, and giving clients more reasons to make referrals.

Why is this vital? In a 2013 survey by *Financial Advisor* magazine, advisors listed the top reason why clients fire advisors as "failure to communicate on a timely basis." Your website can become a key participant in your communication strategy.

Must-Have #9 - I have many reasons to invite prospects to my website.

I can ask them for feedback and point them to the resources that will be valuable for them. As I add resources, such as a complimentary white paper, a new article, a webinar recording, or a "Second Opinion" review, I can announce them to prospects and encourage them to visit my site.

Must-Have #10 - I give centers of influence special invitations.

I introduce them to the resources that would be helpful to their clients (or perhaps themselves). I encourage them to make known to their clients the resources that are available. Also, I take the opportunity to ask centers of influence if they would like print copies of relevant reports and checklists to help their clients with the specific issues and challenges addressed in the reports.

With all ten must-haves in place, your website becomes a hub for your marketing activities.

Another important aspect of packaging is being able to tell your story visually and verbally, especially in introductory meetings. Like a properly tuned instrument, you want to resonate with the correct pitch.

What's Your Pitch? Nine Smart Moves for Your Own Winning Pitch

When you meet with prospects, what's your process for moving your prospects along to saying "Yes!" to taking that next action? In this situation, do you really need a pitch book? Perhaps not. You do, though, need a framework for the journey you and the individual or individuals in front of you will take together. You'll find that framework here in "Nine Smart Moves."

Frequently, financial advisors do rely on a pitch book, often a PowerPoint presentation, when meeting with prospects to determine how or if a relationship would be mutually beneficial. Often advisors add the pitch to their introductory kit or place a printout on the table during a first meeting. First, we'll look at a typical pitch book, and then develop a productive process for that initial meeting. Most often a pitch book attempts too much—to convey a comprehensive picture of everything you do.

One presentation we looked at recently included 43 different slides. Most slides were crammed with text: we counted some 319 words on one slide, and this wasn't unusual. A slide on planning issues listed 15 different topics. Not all slides were meant to be used with any one prospect, but this indiscriminate approach didn't facilitate an optimum outcome.

What can you do differently?

Winding Up for Your Winning Pitch: The Nine Smart Moves

1 - Your presentation is not hit-or-miss. It is built on your foundation of insight into your selected audience and a detailed grasp of your differentiation.

2 - Being selective is a good step for your process with or without a pitch book. Narrow the number of slides or topics to about ten for any one presentation. You are prepared to speak about the details; the slides and text are only a backdrop to your conversation.

3 - Shift the focus from the advisor to the prospect. The title slide needs a prospect-focused headline. If you are concentrating on retirement planning, an example would be "Helping You Live Your Desired Retirement." For a meeting where you have prepared written material only, home in on your prospect in your title. That's your headline. Even if you are working from a bare-bones agenda, you can craft a benefit headline for your prospects.

4 - *Next, you could introduce yourself and your team.* At this point you might have two or three bullet points for each team member (possibly credentials and experience), and you could talk about your passion— why you do what you do.

5 - *Take the prospect on a journey to accomplish that "desired life"* or achieve the benefit you have chosen for your title. Each slide or topic would have short, focused text around which the conversation would flow. Aim for facilitating a conversation, not putting on a one-person show.

6 - *Concentrate fully on your prospect,* noting three of the top challenges to achieving his or her desired life. This opens a conversation that demonstrates your understanding of his or her tough issues and uncovers any specific issues he or she is grappling with.

7 - *Consider describing who you serve.* You could elaborate with a case study that illustrates the problems you address and the advantages achieved. Be aware: this "Who We Serve" section must tie in to the prospect in front of you.

8 - *Choose wisely for additional slides or conversation points.* You could, for example, show how your financial planning process helps to develop your prospect's personal road map. Other slides or conversation points could reveal the outcome of your seven-step investment process and how you collaborate with your prospect, or you could list your key services around a big benefit. Possibly, if relevant, you could add a slide or presentation point about managing downside risk.

9 - *Promote the next step.* Finally, assuming you and your prospect are in sync, the journey's conclusion would lead to the next step, which

you would specifically spell out. Exactly what this step is depends on the needs of the individual in front of you and where he or she is in the client-attracting process.

Notice three important things about this approach:

- It doesn't try to show off your financial smarts with jargon.
- It doesn't brag about how great you and your practice are.
- It doesn't allow PowerPoint to come between you and your audience.

Theodore Roosevelt spoke wisely when he said,
"No one cares how much you know, until they know how much you care."

Your valuable time with your prospect (with or without PowerPoint) is about strengthening that personal connection.

When you are packaging your practice, it is vital to be able to take your different marketing elements and translate them to various media. Because most advisors leverage some form of networking and face-to-face meeting, many communicate their story through a brochure. Do not waste this opportunity.

Calling on a Brochure that Pays Off

Do you really need a brochure? You *don't* if your brochure is going to be just like all but a tiny percentage of brochures.

We received a call for help from Alan after he saw a draft of a three-fold brochure from the firm's usual marketing firm. He felt it was weak, but he couldn't put his finger on what was wrong. The cover featured the firm's logo and George Washington peeking out from behind a dark blue triangle. The logo and design were meant to convey a message, but the reasons why anyone would want to open the brochure were a mystery. Inside, the brochure continued to be all about "we" and "our," only rarely about "you," the prospect. Behind the murky message, though, lurked a story—a story not visible in the brochure.

You do *need a brochure if* your brochure will act as a vibrant, vigorous marketing messenger that produces your desired outcome. Alan's firm combines four professional services: investment, legal, tax, and insurance. The firm wanted to grow by prompting clients or prospects of one service to try out the others for a comprehensive solution. Through the new brochure we created, the firm offered its audience a comprehensive second opinion to "replace a disorganized, piecemeal, and incomplete approach with a comprehensive plan for your future."

Avoid These Three Common Stumbles and Sidestep the Detours and Dead Ends that Can Ambush Your Payoff

Misstep #1. Being unclear about the task you want your brochure to accomplish

Everything follows from this decision. There's much more to a brochure than the satisfaction of simply having one or the fun of showing off a glitzy work of art. If you approach your brochure in a vague, hope-for-the-best way, you'll waste your investment. *How to sidestep this stumble: Have a clear purpose and organize the content from headline to call to action (supported by graphics) to spark that response.*

Misstep #2. Not pinpointing the audience for your brochure

Possibly your audience is a carefully chosen segment of your prospect list. Perhaps you are speaking to prospects for your financial planning services. Or maybe, as Alan's firm did, you would like to motivate prospects to sign up for a second opinion review. *How to sidestep this stumble: Choose a specific job for your brochure to handle for a defined audience.*

Misstep #3. Counting on design to carry your message

Instead, fuel your brochure with proven marketing basics and principles to produce your desired payoff.

Become familiar with the world of your prime audience. Know what they agonize over at night, what frustrates them, and which trends are tearing at their peace of mind. Grasp the fears that are wearing them down day after day. *How to sidestep this stumble: Let your brochure talk about their nagging problems that you can solve. And lace your brochure with benefits important to your audience.*

It comes down to this: A brochure can make a good impression and generate the right response. And the right response is the payoff that you're after. For more ideas check out our *Ten Tips for a Brochure That Really Works* at http://www.marketingplanfinancialadvisor.com/bookresources.html

You are now ready to deliver your Packaging and get your differentiated message in front of your specific audience. In the next chapter on Promoting, you gain marketing strategies, systems, and tactics to reap the results you are looking for by gaining more prospect meetings with better qualified investors and more assets or fees per client.

Promoting
Content Marketing
Meeting Marketing Campaign
White Papers
E-mail
Social Media
Webinars

Chapter 11

P Is for Promoting

"Sell them in bunches, like bananas."
—Tom Hopkins

From a selected list of dozens of marketing programs, tools, and tactics to consider for promoting your practice, here we explore a handful of high-gain tools ranging from an influencer system for referrals through content marketing and webinars.

Unleash the Power of Content Marketing

Today your prospects are more in charge of the advisor selection process than ever before. They are choosing which information to consume, when to do research, who to talk to, how you should and should not communicate with them, and when to get started. At the same time, they face an overload of information and misinformation bellowing for their attention.

In fact, we estimate that 66 percent of prospect research happens before that prospect contacts a financial advisor or firm. Your marketing must reach this majority of your target market before the selection decision happens.

Content marketing is a marketing technique that involves creating and sharing content to attract and engage a clearly defined audience. Its purpose is to drive action. Savvy financial marketers have been using this strategy for decades, and you may know it as two-step or multistep marketing.

> Step 1: Create content, such as a blog article, a free report, a white paper, a webinar, a book, a checklist on your website, or a print or e-mail newsletter. Next, promote your content vigorously through one or more channels such as e-mail, web marketing, direct mail (perhaps a postcard), social media, and others.

> Step 2: Your prospect responds to the action you've asked for in your content. Then you follow up until they become clients (or you drop them from your list). Follow-up can take many forms, including a call, letter, or e-mail (or a sequence of e-mails) to move the prospect to a first meeting.

How Do Financial Advisors Break through the Clatter?

How do they get noticed ahead of competitors and cost-effectively generate and nurture sales leads? Let's turn to Ron's financial advisory practice and how his firm profited from the five R's: the right message to the right people through the right media at the right time for the right results.

Imagine a dream ad that prompts one or two qualified prospects to call you each and every week and request an appointment to meet with you in your office.

Ron's ad, a 30-second radio spot, began with a gut-wrenching question. Not a hit-or-miss attempt, he fine-tuned the ad to connect with his desired audience, empathize with their pain, promote a specific call to action, and add a sense of urgency. In fact, the sense of urgency was so compelling that when prospects called, they often repeated those four almost magical words of urgency from the ad.

The radio ad could have been a postcard to a targeted list, an ad in a local newspaper, a TV commercial, a letter, or something else. Behind the results stood a deep understanding of the advisor's audience of pre-retirees and a development of his differentiation. Simply, the brief radio ad got results because of the marketing commitment that defined Ron's practice.

Be Aware: To truly make a difference, you must leave behind lackluster or one-size-fits-all content. Instead, your content must speed straight to the heart of your designated prospects. If done well, content marketing boosts the impact of your marketing resources.

Five Quick Tips for a Better Content Marketing Strategy

1. **Focus on trends and problems, not only solutions**
   Prospects are twice as likely to move away from problems than move toward a solution. Tap into what gets attention and sales by highlighting through content marketing their gut-wrenching problems that you can solve.

2. **Snag your prospect's attention through snappy headlines**
   One headline can outpull another by 500 percent or more. Prospects have limited attention for your promotion or ad. That's why it is essential to stop them in their tracks through the title of your content and/or the headline or opening of your ad or other marketing communications.

3. **Decide where you engage prospects and which step is next**
   Generally, the bigger the hurdle to jump (such as to pay for a financial plan, fill out a 62-question questionnaire, or bring all your statements to get a detailed analysis of your portfolio), the

more solid the relationship must be or the more you must have built up trust.

4. **Understand the primary types of content and where in the marketing funnel you will use them**

   The three primary categories of content marketing offers, in order of increasing trust required for a response from your target audience, are:

   A. *Something Written* – a blog, white paper, book, free report, guide, checklist, or others.
   B. *An Event or Talk* – a seminar, CD, webinar, workshop, video, or others.
   C. *An Individual Meeting* – a no-obligation consultation, portfolio analysis, get-to-know-you meeting, preretirement review, or others.

5. **Think multimedia, multistep follow-up**

   Today's marketing automation and CRM systems make it easy to set up a follow-up sequence and automate it. Popular sequences include initial lead nurture, meeting request, and cross-sell campaigns with complementary professionals.

Find out more in our checklist *7 Steps to Financial Advisor Content Marketing Success for More Prospect Meetings, AUM, and Clients Now,* which you will find at http://www.marketingplanfinancialadvisor.com/bookresources.html

Next you discover how to take advantage of five productive content marketing strategies:

1. Drive success with your **Meeting Marketing Campaign**
2. Activate growth with **White Papers**

3. Galvanize those on your **E-Mail List** to action
4. Get the most from **Social Media** with a high-level 80/20 strategy
5. Accelerate your results with **webinars**

Drive Success with Your Meeting Marketing Campaign

Whether you are aware of it or not, you are running a one-to-one meeting campaign every time you ask for a meeting, referral, or individual review. So the logical question is, why not "sell them in bunches like bananas" by asking for the meeting in "bunches"? This could be a campaign for an initial meeting or a second opinion review.

Meeting campaigns work if done right. That's a big *if.* Many advisors experience less than one-tenth of a one percent response rate. A response of, say, 3 in 5,000 is a quick way to go broke.

What is the single biggest reason they fail? Most advisor meeting campaigns simply introduce the meeting offer with no benefits, no specifics, no urgency, no buildup of your expertise, and most of all, no history with the list you mail. Too often, it is a cold or suspect list to which you have never mailed before.

No wonder campaigns like these usually bomb.

In contrast, the rural team of Jimmy and James targeted a warm list they had access to. By tying what was going on in the markets and the economy to the reasons for an individual meeting *right away*, they were able to hit a home run with their simple marketing campaign, which yielded a 22 percent response from a simple mailer.

At a minimum, your meeting or second opinion marketing campaign could include a targeted cover letter and a one- to two-page well-prepared brochure. You should answer questions such as these:

-   What problem am I solving (investment performance, no retirement plan, etc.)?
-   Who might benefit from this meeting or review (an investor approaching retirement, etc.)?
-   What is the process I use to deliver results in the second opinion review?
-   Why am I a credible advisor who can give sound advice?
-   What are key benefits of the second opinion review?

It is vital that your meeting campaigns take away the risks that your prospects perceive and get past questions and objections such as:

-   What will I really get out of this meeting? Will I just waste my time?
-   Who is this advisor anyway?
-   Will I get sold something I'll regret buying the minute I walk out of the advisor's office?
-   Who else is doing business with this advisor?
-   Does this advisor really understand me and what I want?
-   I'm not a financial expert; will they talk down to me?
-   Will I feel embarrassed because I don't have answers to their questions?

It comes down to this: *specificity sells*. The more specific you are about your overall process and the more successful you are at taking away fears about your first meeting, the more first meetings you will attract. Now you are in the game and can soar above the din of your prospects' complicated lives for more prospect meetings.

Would you like to discover more about these campaigns and how others have used them to get as high as a 22 percent response from a campaign or add $9 million in assets in a single month? Get *Ten Surefire Ways to Unleash the Power of "Second Opinion" Meeting Marketing for More Clients—Now!* in our Resource Center at http://www.marketingplanfinancialadvisor.com/bookresources.html

Activate Growth with White Papers (Free Reports)

A marketing white paper (or free report) can become your smart first step to generate more qualified prospects, new clients, and assets under management. As a longer marketing communication to draw in your best prospects as leads, it tells the story of how you help individuals just like them solve their pesky problems.

If done right, a white paper can attract the prospects you want and eliminate the frustration of being stuck in pursuit mode. A white paper can transform your sales introduction from a pest to a welcome guest. You can, for instance, gain permission to establish a relationship by presenting your white paper on your website and asking those who are interested to request it there. That's how you catch the attention of prospects early in their research.

What a White Paper Is *Not*

> It is not a watered-down communication with a broad, standard message.
> It is not a sales letter.
> It is not a stock, or generic, article or report that you can use "as is."
> It is not technical proof of your investing style.
> It is not an appeal to anyone and everyone.

Three Elements of a Powerful White Paper to Ensure that It's Done Right

Pin Down with Precision Your Desired Audience: Phil, for example, directed his white paper toward Gen X and Gen Y professionals and mid-career business owners.

Recognize Their Needs and Desires: What are their conflicts? Where is their pain? What do they want least? What do they want most?

Educate Prospects through your Point of View: You have space to reveal your story—to demonstrate exactly how you help people (your top prospects) resolve their baffling dilemmas.

What about length? White papers can be no more than ten pages, including an attractive cover and concluding advisor bio and "About" the firm. They can be digested quickly through headings and subheadings, bullet points, lists, and short sentences and paragraphs, yet if your reader is interested, he or she can peruse your detailed story in about fifteen minutes.

What Can a White Paper Do for Your Financial Advisory Practice?

It can expand the reach of your marketing. You want to be where you can meet a lot of prospects at the right time, generally early in the buying process when they are starting their research. A white paper puts you there.

It can increase the impact of your marketing. You will gain a greater return on the investment of your limited resources. A white paper helps you convert prospects and referrals to clients at a higher rate.

It gives you space to reveal many facets of your unique story.

"Stories aren't the icing on the cake, they are the cake!"
—Peter Guber

It can display your empathy for your audience and illustrate, for instance, how you help clients align their finances with the rest of their lives.

Dorothy created such a white paper for widows, where she told three stories: *a widow's story, a narrative of women's achievements and concerns, and her own story.*

Her white paper began with broad appreciation for women's accomplishments and then narrowed focus to the unique individual holding the white paper in her hand. She probed the top financial challenges women face today from the tough realities of an uncertain economy, the recent market performance (straightforward, without jargon, demonstrating her financial prowess), and both the longevity and inflation risks. Her white paper looked at the emotions women associate with wealth and their topmost aspiration to make the world a better place.

Then she presented her four-step collaborative process to help widows have "a comfortable lifestyle." She took time in her professional bio to connect further by exposing the values she inherited from growing up one of seven children with responsibilities on a ranch.

In a short time, at a prospect's convenience, you appear as someone of substance, expertise, and credibility—someone unlike anyone else, someone worth knowing, someone your prospect can trust. With a white paper you can profit from many of the advantages of writing and publishing a book at a fraction of the investment of time and money. You leave each prospect with a keepsake of who you are and what you can do for him or her.

And there's more. White papers are not only for prospects but also for clients. A year-long Cerulli Associates study found that 70 percent of investors have assets with more than one advisor. The study also discovered that only 17 percent of advisors thought clients kept assets elsewhere. What's an advisor to do? A white paper can clarify your value and boost your chance of gaining more of those assets managed by others.

We invite you to take a look at our checklist *Seven Ways White Papers Can Grow Your Client Base Now.* It's in our Resource Center for you at http://www.marketingplanfinancialadvisor.com/bookresources.html

When capturing a lead with content marketing, you will want to get the e-mail address of your prospects. And virtually every advisor today uses e-mail as the primary communication with clients.

Galvanize Those on Your E-Mail List to Action

How many e-mails do you receive in a day *not* counting spam? For many it is a hundred (or more) day after day after day ... enough to be overwhelming. That's why you are cautious about what you sign up for and selective about which e-mails you pay attention to. We see common financial advisor stumbles when calling on e-mail as a marketing tool.

Misstep #1 – Trying to build your prospect list by expecting people to hand over contact information on your website just because you have a sign-up box for a newsletter

Why should they clutter their lives with one more humdrum e-mail series? Your sign-up box says nothing about the value people receive. Suppose, though, you gave them an incentive to sign up, such as a special report or white paper that solves a problem that grabs them and won't let go. There you will provide answers that will make their lives better, easier, or happier.

Misstep #2 – Not putting your *all* into your e-mail subject

How many people on your list will be enticed by a subject line that says "Read My Blog Post"? More will stop in their tracks to find out what is inside with a subject line such as "Something Big Going on That You Aren't Reading About."

Much of the power of the 2012 Obama campaign and most of the $690 million raised online came from e-mails. The 8 to 20 e-mail writers, working each day as long as they could stay awake, tested everything.

You can bet that the subject line was never an afterthought. The writers discovered that what worked best were informal phrases that you might see from people you know. Then it's up to you to immediately follow up on the promise of your subject line in your first sentence.

Misstep #3 – Isolating your e-mail from your other marketing tools

Here's one example of how to harmonize e-mail with direct mail. Perry Marshall, the AdWords guru, is a welcome guest. Shirley has met him at web marketing conferences and bought his books, courses, and mentoring programs. His e-mail messages, though, don't always stop her in her tracks in the midst of a tight schedule and an overload of e-mails. She wasn't aware of an upcoming webinar. Guess what compelled her to attend? A postcard from Perry announcing his webinar on the secrets of higher landing-page conversion.

Now let's look at how social media might be used strategically to grow your practice.

Get the Most from Social Media with a High-Level 80/20 Strategy

Some advisors see social media marketing as a quick and easy solution for practice growth. Few, though, have found social media to be their marketing cure-all. A common error we find is that advisors sign up willy-nilly for popular social media options and display their links on their websites and other communications. Then they wait for a payoff.

What does it mean to be strategic?

A survey of more than 3000 marketers in the "2013 Social Media Marketing Industry Report," with its 70 charts, goes only so far in guiding you through the social media maze. And, of course, the survey doesn't deal with a financial advisor's regulatory requirements.

On the list were the top six most commonly used social media selections: Facebook, Twitter, LinkedIn, Blogging, YouTube, and Google+ ("on the radar for many marketers"). Yet that's not the first of your considerations about your social media strategy as you carefully pin down how you want to invest your resources. You must grasp what you want social media to do for you. Social media can help advisors intensify relationships with current clients, draw on the resources of thought leaders to fuel your growth, share meaningful content (yours and others), build credibility with prospects and influencers, and more.

Social media marketing is not static. We see upstarts surface and established media surge ahead or fade. Before you decide where to invest in social media:

- Select your audience for your social media campaign,
- Understand your marketing objectives for social media,
- Determine the best way to reach your audience,

- Decide how you can integrate social media into your existing or new marketing campaigns, and
- Weigh the costs.

Once you make these decisions, then we invite you to follow these four steps for a strategic approach to social media.

1 – Make a smart choice for yourself and your practice

Whether you are already participating in social media or are about to decide where you can best invest your resources, it's vital to focus on where your audience gravitates. Our own surveys in 2013 of small businesspeople and professionals indicate that 70 percent plan on using LinkedIn as a part of their social media mix. If professionals or the small business audience are included in your centers of influence or prospecting efforts, LinkedIn could make sense.

2 – Plan on a long-term relationship

Realize that you can't set your social media campaign once and forget it.

✓ Success demands time in the sense of scheduling time to devote each day or each week to social media.

✓ Results require a dialogue—sharing something of yourself (not generic content) and sharing something from others. Educate, enlighten, and engage to build your following.

✓ A payoff also calls for time in the sense of waiting after you launch your marketing campaign until you start seeing real results in your book of business.

3 – Hold realistic expectations

The two top benefits that the 3000+ marketers revealed in the "2013 Social Media Marketing Industry Report" are increased exposure and increased traffic to their websites. Both of these advantages can produce qualified leads, but it may not happen right away.

4 – Integrate your social media approach with content marketing

Be strategic by calling on social media to boost the power of a new marketing campaign or to enhance what is already working for you. Thoughtful content is vital. It starts with your website—not just any website but one that will enhance your social media presence. See the section above with *Ten Must-Haves for a Website that Wins Clients.*

Consider: Social media can be effective both for fortifying your networking and building up your book of business. Combining your social media selection with a productive content marketing program can yield new centers of influence and clients and also add assets, just as it has for some advisors.

Accelerate Your Results with Webinars

> "Webinars are the greatest unsung heroes of marketing."
> —Frank Kern

Webinars have leveled the playing field so that any financial practice or advisor can appear to be the market leader. You can replace an expensive seminar program, which typically involves direct mail, a room, and a meal, with a virtual seminar room and no food, plus the advantage of inexpensive e-mail and social marketing.

Our studies show that the cost of a prospect lead through webinars is roughly five times cheaper than in-person marketing seminars. And while a maximum of one in four prospects would consider attending a seminar as a part of the buying process, roughly six in ten would attend a live webinar or watch an on-demand recording.

Webinars combine visual elements delivered from your computer (such as a Microsoft PowerPoint presentation) with, most often, a teleseminar delivered through a phone bridge or the computer speakers. Attendees are in listen-only mode, as if they were listening to a speaker at an in-person seminar. Also, technology allows attendees to ask questions via text to interact with the webinar presenters.

And perhaps most beneficial, live webinars can be easily recorded and viewed on demand by prospects. Through your website you can make the recording available at all times.

Why Webinars for Financial Advisors?

Like many other types of events, these one-to-many online events can accomplish vital objectives. Advisors can generate new prospect leads, help convert prospects to clients, and reveal your story and personality directly to prospects.

Top Tips for Profitable Webinars

Bob's experience over more than a dozen years and countless events has stirred up results from webinars. Jerry gained $1 million in committed AUM in six days after his first prospect webinar. Trevor, a new advisor, had been able to engage prospects in "good conversations" with many contacts, but found it tough to sign up clients in his first year. Within 90 days of his initial webinar, he converted four of these prospects into new clients.

A third advisor, Carl, saved hundreds of hours per year by turning individual quarterly meetings with clients into quarterly market update and analysis webinars. By freeing this time for marketing, he grew his practice from roughly $110 million under management to $200 million in four years after this switch, and he was able to spend less time at the office.

Here are key steps in getting the results you're looking for from webinars.

Decide on your audience

Is your number one audience prospects, current clients, or COIs (centers of influence)? The majority of your prospective clients, for example, will tend to be found earlier in the selection process. But most financial advisors have not recognized this and don't have a marketing strategy to engage the many potential early-stage prospects and then nurture those prospects to become clients.

Clarify your purpose

This is the foundation for everything that follows. Know precisely what you would like to happen as the outcome of your webinar. Remember, generally the narrower the objectives for a webinar, the more likely it is to succeed.

Select your topic strategically

The webinar topic is the most important factor prospective attendees value when making a choice to register for a webinar. Topics that promise to deliver value to your selected target audience will have the best chance to pull in that audience. For example, a market or economic update may work very well with existing clients; an overview of retirement planning will draw in prospects; and a technical discussion of a financial specialty will tend to attract professional COIs.

Mix media to invite your audience

E-mail invitations are, by far, the most effective promotional channel to recruit webinar attendees, with the use of social media on the rise. Websites, newsletters, ads, call campaigns, and direct mail are other ways advisors promote webinars.

Plan a series of contacts to attract your audience

Once is never enough. Generate a sequence of contacts to drive registrants, convert registrants into attendees, and promote the webinar recording.

Craft a presentation with staying power

Wise advice comes from Chris Anderson, curator of TED (Technology, Entertainment, Design) conferences. According to TED attendees, *content* with specific actionable items is essential in keeping them engaged throughout the webinar. *Context,* also, is of critical importance because attendees value a presenter who uses stories and examples to illustrate facts. Simply sharing market or economic data without a context is ranked relatively low in importance.

Anderson adds, "Play to your strengths and give a talk that is truly authentic to you."

Prepare for your presentation with serious intent

Try to get beyond reading scripts. If you use PowerPoint, keep it simple and don't just recite what you've put on the screen. Avoid providing too much information on a single slide and steer clear of complex charts. Call on available interaction opportunities to further engage your audience.

Put a follow-up plan into play to shepherd your audience to your desired outcome

A multistep plan will drive through the clutter of your audience's busy life. An e-mail with a link to the webinar recording, as well as a specific promotion of your first meeting mixed with a call or two, can be a tremendously powerful conversion sequence.

Remember, it's never over until it's over. Your webinar is easily recorded and marketed through e-mail, your website, social media, and other media. You can take advantage of this asset for months, or even years, to see as much as a doubling of viewers over live webinars alone.

Next, we look at a strategic approach to unlock the power of referrals from centers of influence and clients.

Gain Traction
Referrals from Clients
More Referrals through Influencers

Chapter 12

Gain Traction through the World of Referrals and Influencers

"The system works so you don't have to."
—Michael Gerber, Author of *The E-Myth*

Years ago Bob Hanson realized the power of this system for winning in his marketplace by identifying complementary (noncompetitive) firms that were marketing and selling to his prospects. He developed the system when he worked for a small, little-known firm with many big-name, big-marketing-budget competitors. "I saw how quickly productive relationships with those influential with your target market can build a business by generating a steady flow of prospects," he said.

"How about 2,245 prospects at one event without spending a dime on marketing? I did that while helping to build a 70,000-name marketing list and increase sales fourfold in just over 36 months. There is strength in this marketing strategy, *if done right*. And that's why I want to help you end the frustration of influencer systems that don't work."

For example, Monty, a solo advisor who wanted to reach high net worth prospects on a small budget, partnered with three other firms on his first in-person event to target millionaires. The outcome: 76 prospects showed up for three hours on a Saturday morning in the middle of a scorching summer heat wave.

Financial advisors continue to grapple with effective ways to attract new clients. This area is a tough one for advisors. A recent *InvestmentNews/* Moss Adams survey found that 61 percent of new clients come from referrals, yet most firms do not have a formal referral process. *Financial Advisor* magazine surveyed 611 advisors and found that the prime source for new clients was from client referrals. However, the best new clients in terms of "most profitable" came from centers of influence. But only 10 percent report "having very much success."

> Audrey, a financial advisor, tried scattershot referral marketing. She brings impressive credentials to her work—both a CPA and a CFP® along with more than 24 years of financial services experience. She serves on the boards of a local hospital and local college and was the first woman elected to the board of her country club.
>
> Imagine the qualified prospects in her network! Yet she is getting "very little business" from her efforts.

This outcome—little to show for a large commitment—is not unusual. An informal survey by Red Zone Marketing revealed that only about 1 percent of financial advisors said that networking worked for them.

Before we go ahead with the exact steps you need for a productive centers of influence system, we would like to explore a path to more referrals from clients.

Boost Referrals from Clients with Your Six-Point Plan

Your six-point plan for a referral network can generate a whole lot more than 12 new clients a year (from 12 client referrers and one client or more from each one at a minimum).

1 - Identify Referral Sources

Generally 80 percent of your referrals will come from 20 percent of your referral sources. So identify those few who will yield the most results and cultivate those relationships.

2 - Approach Them with Your Referral Pitch or Process

Remember, just sending a letter or asking is not good enough: you need to prepare the ground for conditions that are productive and ask in a way that gets results. Follow the Nine-Step Road Map that you find below and include as "influencers" your clients who will make referrals.

3 - Make It Easy for People to Refer, and Take Control of the Process

This is often where advisors stumble and lose out on the most referrals. Obviously you should not assign the client you hope will make a referral the task of "giving the prospect my card" or "getting my video to them." It's *unlikely* to happen.

You can better take control of the process by making sure you get the prospect's contact info up front and approach potential clients over time with a combination of the following. The referred prospect can call for an appointment, receive a free report, subscribe to your newsletter, receive an event invitation, or get a coupon for a no-obligation portfolio review.

4 - Follow Up with the Referrals and Convert Them to Clients

Usually a one-time contact is not enough. Multiple follow-ups using multiple media over a short period of time (within 30 days of the initial contact) are best. These can include:

- sending an e-mail, intro letter, or package,
- calling, and
- inviting the referred prospect to hear a recorded talk or live event.

5 - Reward Clients for Referrals

Your appreciation can be both formal with thank-you gifts, perhaps with a restaurant card, or better, with a gift that reflects your client's hobbies or passions, or an informal handwritten thank-you note. Your gratitude will encourage future referrals. (Keep your gifts within any compliance limits.)

6 - Repeat the Process with Each of Your Top Referring Clients at Least Annually

An option is to try out the referral survey process. An established advisor, Tim, had no luck with a video that he sent out to key sources hoping they would pass it along to prospects they knew. Once he tried the survey, he received nine quality referrals right away. You will find the *Sample Referral Survey Process* at http://www.marketingplanfinancialadvisor.com/bookresources.html

The influencer system that follows is an alternative to the hope-for-the-best, Hail Mary play approach. It is the solution to low-gain networking and referral attempts. Keep in mind that some 80 percent of your introductions will come from about 20 percent of your advocates, regardless of the type. So having a system for introductions and/or leveraging relationships with those who influence your target market will put the 80/20 principle to work to fuel your practice growth.

Your Financial Influencer Marketing System

A financial influencer marketing system can be described simply as getting others to market for you and sell prospects on your practice. Your system encompasses:

- Getting referrals from clients,
- Getting referrals from other businesses or professionals,
- Getting referrals from your network,
- Co-Marketing (doing marketing together) with other parties with one-shot marketing,
- Sponsoring others' marketing events or programs,
- Co-marketing with wholesalers or distributors,
- Creating ongoing marketing programs with others,
- Developing a strategic business relationship with another firm or firms,
- Leveraging your content marketing engine to warm lists and leads,
- And more.

The system is repeatable, scalable, and measurable. It does *not* require ongoing heavy lifting, but instead basic care and feeding once it is in place.

The secret is to establish a two-way relationship with other professionals and those who are influential or marketing and selling to your target market.

Two-way is *not* about asking for referrals and expecting referrals in return. Two-way means a shared and collaborative relationship. How can you help the other professionals? This is a critical question too often missed. As a starter, you can help them see your value by educating them about the services you provide (a white paper does this very well). That way, you could become the solution to a puzzling situation the professional's client faces. Perhaps she's a new widow whose husband's advisor discounted her. She knows she doesn't want to work with that dismissive advisor, but she doesn't know where to turn.

A shy advisor, Chris, found a practice management consultant who targeted the same dentists he did in the region. Chris sponsored the consultant's quarterly workshop (where the consultant did virtually all the talking) and garnered two to three high-quality prospect meetings from each event with virtually zero exertion and minimal expense.

The Nine-Step Road Map to Attract More Referrals and Clients through Influencers

We invite you to follow these nine steps for more productive influencer relationships, more referrals, and more clients:

1 - Target your "A" clients and influencers
2 - Qualify potential influencers at the first meeting
3 - Communicate your IVP, "Influencer Value Proposition"
4 - Market through influencers—list and media
5 - Market through influencers—make a compelling offer
6 - Market through influencers with effective communications/ marketing copy
7 - Convert leads to meetings and clients
8 - Carry out your referral system
9 - Build on success.

To help you create your financial influencer system, we designed an easy-to-follow process that virtually anyone can use and profit from. It's time to spotlight these nine heavy-duty steps one by one.

1 - Target Your "A" Clients and Influencers

The key to getting more of your ideal clients is knowing who those clients are before you seek them out or ask others to help you recruit them. You'll find everything you need in chapter 7, "Getting into Your Growth Groove: Ideal Client Discovery."

It comes down to targeting your "A" clients and influencers by:

- Knowing who your "A" clients are and being able to describe them in detail,
- Knowing who your potential influencers are by developing your ideal influencer criteria,
- Understanding how you can help "A" clients and potential influencers, and
- Being able to find them.

2 - Qualify Potential Influencers at the First Meeting

Many financial professionals do a first-rate job of setting up plenty of meetings with potential influencers, but they fail to achieve any referrals or results and suffer frustration. Too often, they sabotage success by their pitch. The financial advisor is, in effect, throwing himself or herself at the potential influencer with little thought given to the nine-step road map.

Here we offer a framework to get more results from the first meeting and ultimately more clients from this system. You may be surprised to hear that Bob favors doing these meetings by phone or web because (1) you get more first meetings this way and (2) generally it is easier to get down to business.

Consider the following three goals from a typical first networking or potential influencer meeting:

1. Position yourself with your value proposition,
2. Qualify the potential influencer using your ideal influencer criteria, and
3. Outline and agree to the next steps in the relationship.

Make sure to qualify your potential influencer by asking key questions such as: Are you open to new relationships? What experience have you had in referring clients? This question is important because if the influencer has not referred others, it is doubtful that he or she will act on your behalf. Or for co-marketing relationships, what types of clients/prospects/relationships do you have today and what type of marketing do you do now?

Also, especially if the first meeting seems to be ending with no immediate next steps, assuming you have done a good job of communicating your Influencer Value Proposition (see the next step), don't be afraid to ask for introductions to other potential centers of influence then and there.

3- Prepare and Promote Your "IVP" or Influencer Value Proposition

You are doing business in a tough environment of indistinguishable competing firms where people are more skeptical, confused, and mistrustful than ever. How can you stand out from the pack? To get started with your Influencer Value Proposition, answer these five questions. Then be ready to summarize them in a paragraph or two in your next meeting with a potential influencer.

1. Who do you target (your list of "A" clients)?
2. What problems of theirs do you solve and how do you solve them uniquely?
3. What few key facts build your credibility?
4. How do you help your influencers (your shared vision of success)?
5. *What are big potential benefits for them of working with you?*

Following are three vital steps to success in marketing through influencers: the list or media, the offer, and the marketing copy.

4 - Market through Influencers—List and Media

> In real estate everyone knows it's "location, location, location."
> In marketing it's "the list, the list, the list."

No matter what offer you present and how well you present it, the list or media you use will almost always be the most important factor in the success of your marketing campaigns. This is why influencer marketing—marketing through others—is so powerful!

What is your best list? "Best list" means a list where you already have a favorable relationship with the people on it. Yes, that would be your own list. *The optimum long-term strategy is to do what you have to do to generate your own opt-in database. And always gain permission.*

Your next candidate for your "best list" will be your influencer's client and prospect list, especially if they have many people who fit your "A" prospect profile. Investing extra time to make sure your influencer has the right list for you is time well spent.

Warning: Use only an opt-in list for e-mail—one where people gave permission to receive information via e-mail. That means never contact people on a list that's compiled from websites, Twitter comments, and so on. You may unleash a venomous backlash against you.

5 - Market through Influencers—Make a Compelling Offer

Your offer is what your prospect gets for responding. The offer is most often, but not always, free. Questions to answer about your offer include:

- Is my offer something we can deliver on?
- Does the offer solve a big problem or promise a big benefit to my target audience?
- Is this information my target market wants to hear?

- Will those who respond to the offer be predisposed to buy my products/services if they like the information presented in the offer?
- Are we putting our best foot forward for the offer by describing it in a persuasive way?

6 - Market through Influencers with Effective Communications/ Marketing Copy

Where your offer and copy first intersect is in the title or subject of your offer. Be sure the title of your written piece, the subject or title of your seminar, webinar, or event, or the name for your meeting is compelling to your target audience. "Unleash the Power of Content Marketing" in chapter 11 goes into greater detail about offers.

In selecting the "right words" to get your prospects to respond, concentrate on:

1) The headline/subject/title,
2) The main copy with relevant benefits, and
3) Your call to action to prompt prospects to respond.

See *Your Power Checklist: 20 Tips to Help You Write Copy Like a Marketing Wizard* at http://www.marketingplanfinancialadvisor.com/ bookresources.html

7 - Convert Leads to Clients and Fees

A survey by our CRM vendor of its clients revealed that some had experienced a 400 percent increase in new business. The only difference was that their successful clients constantly followed up with the leads and prospects they were generating.

What not to do: Do not leave the follow-up of your referrals and influencers to chance. Take control of the process to make sure that what should happen does take place.

8 - Carry Out Your Referral System

Here we weigh in with five keys to success with your referral system:

1. Educate influencers to appreciate your value and know who your ideal prospect is.
2. Ask for the referral and take control by getting the name and contact information at that time.
3. Put the referral into your automated follow-up marketing or sales process.
4. Track results and keep unconverted prospects on your list for ongoing contacts.
5. Repeat this system at least annually for "A" and "B" clients and prime influencers.

9 - Build on Success

Once your system is in place, don't stop. An influencer system that produces happy results and flows forward on its own momentum will help you constantly grow and expand.

It comes down to this: Know what you want your influencer system to be, understand your target market, grasp how you can help potential influencers, and *act!*

If you are like most advisors, you have gotten better in your role—more experienced, more in tune with your target clients, and better poised for growth. *There has likely never been a better time to break through to the next level.*

Perhaps in the past you leveraged only one tactic to get prospects. Possibly it performed for you slowly and steadily. We invite you to try these two simple steps:

Step 1 - Make improvements on your first tactic and

Step 2 - Add a second tactic to your current source of business that can unleash your growth potential.

We recommend that you take a serious look at our centers of influence system for the marketing tool you add. Suppose you broaden your definition of influencers beyond estate attorneys and CPAs to those who have influence over your target audience and are already marketing and selling to that market. Suppose, also, that you follow the straightforward centers of influence system we spelled out for you. *Those steps can unlock your vision for your practice.*

Conclusion

"The Best Way to Predict Your Future Is to Create It." —Peter F. Drucker

Now that you have everything at your fingertips for marketing results, we don't want anything to derail your success. Research findings reveal that you have a greater chance of reaching your goals if you add specific actions that need to be taken. That's a way to snatch marketing out of that "important but never urgent" category (identified by Stephen Covey) and put it front and center.

What are *your* goals for your practice? How specific are they? If they are general, you will fall short. We invite you to call on these three specific marketing goals to propel you into action:

1. Dedicate a certain number of hours at the office every week to strategic projects such as marketing. Also, make sure to set aside selling time for new prospects.

2. Integrate your marketing strategy into a system so that it happens automatically and needs little care and feeding. Call on technology, repeatable marketing processes, and an assistant (where possible) who can help make marketing happen for you.

3. Generate and follow a 90-day marketing calendar and keep it updated.

What Difference Would You See in Your Practice if You Benefited from the Strategies, Tools, and Tactics You Discovered Here?

Richard, a client, answers. In the *Planning* process he identified and tuned into his target clients—their dreams and the problems rocking their lives. A fascinating 2010 Hinge Marketing Research Study of "High Growth Professional Services Firms" (including financial firms) concluded, "The more they looked into their target clients' needs, the faster they grew and the more profitable they were." What's more, Richard crafted his strong, easy-to-understand differentiation and spelled out how he improves the lives of his selected audience.

For his core communications, his *Packaging*, Richard developed a website that explores his specialness through the eyes of his target audience. For prospect meetings he built a sharply focused ten-slide pitch book. Also, he called on a brochure that centers on his target audience. He concentrated his *Promoting* resources on tools that would accelerate his growth, such as a strategic referrals strategy and content marketing through a white paper. What were his results?

This could be you: Revenues grew by 30 percent in 2013, and Richard is seeing strong growth again this year.

Don't waste another day with a practice that is anything less than you desire. Start creating your future now. To get more information on how we might help you turn your vision into reality with group coaching and success tools or custom marketing services, coaching, and writing, **we invite you to talk with Bob Hanson at 617-901-6886 or go to www.marketingplanfinancialadvisor.com**

About the Authors

Bob Hanson, President of Quantum Leap Marketing, Inc. is a partner in the Client-Attraction Marketing System for Financial Advisors. He is skilled in helping advisors generate growth by developing their distinct marketing system. His comprehensive approach begins with planning. From there he helps advisors generate effective, custom marketing programs designed to produce at least one new ideal client a month, each and every month

He has personally interviewed over 1,000 financial advisors to investigate what works and what does not work when it comes to practice growth and marketing. Also, he has worked directly with hundreds of advisors and advisory teams of all types with diverse investment philosophies and in various stages of experience. The outcome: They are able to get in front of more target prospects, differentiate their practice, and multiply clients and assets.

While in college he discovered marketing leverage and its almost unlimited upside. In his more than 22 years of experience with hands-on, results-focused marketing, he has helped create $1.45 billion in quantified sales opportunities for a single firm, has grown revenues for another four-fold in 36 months, and helped grow a website consulting firm from 5 to 850 people within 18 months before filing for an IPO. Over the last 10 years he has devoted much of his time to helping financial advisors and practices multiply prospect flow, assets, and income.

He got an early start in high school by creating his own futures trading system. His first formal introduction in the industry came through an internship at Kidder, Peabody & Co. in 1988. His clients over the years have varied from broker dealers, RIAs, financial technology and CRM firms, financial media, CPAs and other wealth management professionals, venture capital firms, and countless individual wirehouse and independent advisors.

He earned an M.B.A. from the F.W. Olin School at Babson College and a B.A. from Tufts University. He has authored dozens of articles, reports, and success guides on marketing and has ghostwritten numerous articles and white papers on investing, planning, and financial products. This is his first book.

Bob lives in the Greater Boston area with his family.

Shirley Hanson is a partner in the Client-Attraction Marketing System for Financial Advisors. Since her discovery of direct marketing in 1990, she has zeroed in on what works and what doesn't work. Her journey took her through trial-and-error experience, books and online resources, intense coaching programs with marketing and copywriting maestros, strenuous boot camps, and interactions with clients.

Shirley lives in the remarkable community of Chestnut Hill, Philadelphia, where writing for the local newspaper and training in community renewal led to a Master of City Planning degree from the University of Pennsylvania. Both planning and writing are skills she brings to her clients. Her first book was the classic in its field, *Preserving and Maintaining the Older Home* (Mc-Graw Hill). Today as a volunteer she raises funds for non-profits and helps to protect historic resources and conserve open space.

For the past 15 years she has enabled financial advisors to take advantage of the same strategies and tactics that high-growth firms count on year after year to efficiently activate their growth. She rescues advisors from an all-things-to-all-people approach to generate true differentiation. She steers them away from hit-or-miss marketing programs that waste resources. Also, she takes the hassle out of writing brochures, creating content for websites, and producing articles or special reports. The result of her coaching, copywriting, and consulting: Advisors are able to break through to the level of growth they desire.

Selected Bibliography

Clifton, Donald O. and Nelson, Paula, *Soar with Your Strengths: A Simple Yet Revolutionary Philosophy of Business and Management.* New York: The Random House Publishing Group, 1992 and 2010.

Collins, James C. and Porras, Jerry I, "Building Your Company's Vision. *Harvard Business Review,* September 1996.

Covey, Stephen M.R., *The Speed of Trust: The One Thing That Changes Everything.* New York: Free Press, a division of Simon & Schuster, Inc., 2008.

Gelb, Michael J., *Discover Your Genius: How to Think Like History's Ten Most Revolutionary Minds.* New York: HarperCollins Publishers, Inc., 2002.

Koch, Richard, *The 80/20 Principle: The Secret to Success by Achieving More With Less.* New York: Doubleday, 1998.

Trout, Jack, *Trout on Strategy: Capturing Mindshare, Conquering Markets.* New York: McGraw-Hill, 2004.